Compositions: Notes on the written word

Compositions:
Notes on the written word

Naomi Beth Wakan

Wolsak and Wynn

Author's photograph: Elias Wakan, www.eliaswakan.com
Cover Image: Elias Wakan, www.eliaswakan.com
Book design: Julie McNeill, McNeill Design Arts

The publishers gratefully acknowledge the support of the Canada Council for the Arts, the Ontario Arts Council and the Book Publishing Industry Development Program (BPIDP) for their financial assistance.

The Canada Council | Le Conseil des Arts
for the Arts | du Canada

ONTARIO ARTS COUNCIL
CONSEIL DES ARTS DE L'ONTARIO

Canadian   Patrimoine
Heritage   canadien

Wolsak and Wynn Publishers Ltd
69 Hughson Street North, Ste. 102
Hamilton, ON
Canada L8R 1G5
www.wolsakandwynn.ca

Unless otherwise attributed, all poetry in *Compositions: Notes on the Written Word* is by Naomi Beth Wakan. Many of the poems appear in *Segues*, (Wolsak and Wynn, 2005).

Library and Archives Canada Cataloguing in Publication

Wakan, Naomi
Compositions : notes on the written word / Naomi Beth Wakan.

ISBN 978-1-894987-25-7

I. Title.

PS8595.A547Z463 2008   C814'.54   C2008-901129-5

To Dr. Alice Weaver Flaherty
– whom I have just met

Contents

Foreword

Since this is a book of essays, perhaps I should first explain why I like this form of writing so much. I am not a linear-minded person. My mind likes to twist and turn its way home, and for such a mind, the essay is the perfect way to express its thoughts. The essay allows me to meander. It allows me to stop here and there to consider more deeply some vantage point. The essay encourages me to adventure down some side road that may, or may not, rejoin the main. If it doesn't, I often find myself in a mess of brambles through which I have to scramble in order to get back to the theme. The end of the essay, surprisingly enough, usually finds me somewhere close to its beginning. Ever hopeful, I can only trust that I, and my readers, have profited somewhat from the journey.

It seems strange to me now that my first introduction to essays as a young girl was 18th century essays – Joseph Addison and Sir Richard Steele in *The Spectator* and *The Tatler;* the latter with its motto *quicquid agunt homines nostri farrago libelli,* Juvenal's telling that "whatever people do shall form the mixed subject of my paper." Or, as Professor Giulietta Campari so quaintly puts it, "Whatever man do, or say, or think, or dream, our motley paper seizes for its theme."

Later *The Spectator* took up the same aim as *The Tatler,* and Addison observed, "I shall leave it to my Reader's consideration, whether it is not much better to be let into the knowledge of one's self, than to hear what passes in Muscovy or Poland; and to amuse ourselves with such writings as tend to the wearing out of ignorance, passion and prejudice, than such as naturally conduce to inflame hatreds, and make enmities irreconcilable." I was inspired by such thoughts from these early writers. The whole idea of writing personally of small, local matters in a non-aggressive manner was to become the aim of much of my later writing.

As a school girl I found *The Tatler* and *Spectator's* commentaries on early 18th century society witty and entrancing. Now, I'm sure that on rereading they would no longer be so thrilling, but enthral me they did at the time, and I followed their reading with the essays of Charles Lamb, Hilaire Belloc and G.K.Chesterton.

Michel de Montaigne had laid it all out earlier when he told how he, "took the first subject that chance offers; they are all equally good to me. And I never purpose to treat them exhaustively." Fine, I like to skim over and around themes as well, so I took Montaigne's example as my model. It was Montaigne who in 1580 first used the word 'essay;' the word derived from the French, *essayer*, to attempt. Nassan Nicholas Taleb recently expanded on the idea of an essay as an attempt, when he said, "The very word *essay* conveys the tentative, the speculative, and the non-definitive … an impulse meditation." Tentative and unsystematic best describe my 'attempts,' making me a very humble follower in Montaigne's footsteps.

Charles Cornwallis later expounded, in a similar way, on the subject of an essay, "A Gentleman should talk like a Gentleman, which is, like a wise man. His knowledge ought to be general: it becomes him not to talk of one thing too much or to be weighed down with any particular profession … One knowledge is but one part of a house, a bay-window or a gable-end. Who builds his house so maimed, much less himself? No, be complete." Complete I'm not, but I can expound on many aspects of my house.

After my school days, there seems to have been a hiatus in my essay reading while I universitied, married and emigrated to the Americas. My loyalties then swung sharply to the members of the Algonquin Round Table and authors such as James Thurber, Dorothy Parker and Robert Benchly. I wished I could join their ranks, sans all that drinking and those suicide attempts. After settling in Canada, I added Stephen Leacock and for a little more dignity, George Woodcock, to my list of essayists. Later the nature essayists, Anne Dillard, Diane Ackerman and the merry-go-round science essayist, James Burke, in his 'Connections' column in *Scientific American,* were appended to my essay-reading list.

Taking up my schoolgirl pencil again in my sixties, I opted for compositions again. Compositions, for after all isn't that just what an essay is – a school-child's composition? My compositions were on topics that I could use as an excuse-hook on which to hang my opinion-hat and my vantage-cloak. Many of these essays were on the writing process, which was starting to envelope my life, and out of them came *Late Bloomer: On Writing Later in Life.* Here, as a sequel, is *Compositions* – a gathering of musings on books, writers and writing.

Begin
at the
Beginning

The Originating Point

I am a writer-cum-artist-cum-dilettante and work in a vinyl-sided cottage on the small island of Gabriola, in the Georgia Strait, British Columbia. My husband, the wood sculptor Elias Wakan, and I work, each in our own isolation, at a fairly steady pace throughout the year and only open our studio to the public when the spirit moves us. For example, the other day I merely went out onto the porch to see if the daffodils had lifted their heads yet, when I found myself, for no conscious reason, removing the closed notice from our Drumberg House Studio sign.

The daffodils had not yet lifted their heads. But I also noted that a car had drawn to a halt outside our house and that a man was emerging. I greeted him and he said that he would like to view the studio. He turned out to be a psychologist. Nothing so strange about that, people often use our studio to reveal different layers of their being, many times without being invited to do so. What was interesting was that he was, he said, exploring the 'creative process.' Even though I suppose I have been consciously part of this process for the last twenty years, it has always remained a mystery to me, even when I was swirling around in its midst, so his focus intrigued me.

My surname is an acquired name. My husband and I chose it together for ourselves when we were getting married. I often hear myself explaining our surname, 'Wakan,' to visitors. "It is a Sioux Native word meaning 'creative spirit,'" I say. "For example, when a potter makes a fine pot, the pot has 'wakan,' and if he makes a series of fine pots, then he has 'wakan' moving through him." Choosing the name was an aspiration for both of us and, I suppose, for the marriage itself. I think the choice was the first step to us becoming self-consciously creative.

But back to the psychologist and his creative yearnings. As I entered the studio, he turned to me and asked what I thought the creative process was. I was ready for daffodils, but I was not ready for definitions that early in the day. I squirmed a bit and told him that an 'Aha' moment always indicated to me that a creative act had been, was, or will be about to take place. This just spilled out of me involuntarily and unwillingly, inviting him to probe further, as psychologists often do. And he did so by asking, "But where does the 'Aha!' thing come from?"

Never lost for words, even though I sometimes do not know what they are going to be, I thought I responded rather smartly. I explained that although I do not know its source, the 'Aha!' moment means that a connection has been made and that connection has allowed me to see something in a fresh way. I gave him Gutenberg as an example, for he saw a winepress and a punch press, everyday things, but he saw them connected as a printing press.

Sometimes, when an 'Aha!' moment occurs, I try to ground it by turning its energy into a poem, an essay or a knitted scarf. These may not be particularly original creations, but most of them do seem to have a fresh element that adds a positive note to the way I see the world turning.

No matter how deeply our caller might ask me about this 'creative spirit,' or, indeed, how intensely I had explored the creative act in the past, the originating point of creativity always seems to disappear into the mist. Many would say that

'God' is the initiator, and indeed, the artist has been described by M. B. Goffstein, as "like God, but small." Arthur Koestler said that the creative act could be described as a type of learning process where teacher and pupil are located in the same individual. And while it is true that I talk about "my ideas," I must admit that they seem also not to come from me at the same time that I claim them.

As the mystery of the creative source deepens, it paradoxically appears to me that almost any everyday event can become a creative act. It seems to me that intensity and intent is what makes an act creative. Still, I look at my husband's letterhead logo from time to time. It is all there ... the point, the line, the flat surface and the solid three dimensional figure. Four images that describe how his ideas are translated into wood. But they do not *explain* it. And the void, from which all apparently manifests, still remains a paradox. The Jewish mystics hint at a level behind, or beyond, this void, which they call *Adam Kadmon,* but as they indicate that 'nothing can be properly thought or said' of the void, this even farther-back source of creative energy seems equally impossible to grasp.

I find that I have thought all this aloud, for the psychologist is now fixing me with some attention, although he is not taking notes. (I hate it when people don't take notes when I think they should. Eli and I are great readers and each keep our 50 allotted book reserves allowed by the library filled to the top. When visitors suggest titles that have impressed them, we duly note them down and order them from the library. I am mildly annoyed when no one else seems to record and request my recommendations in that respectful way.)

Ever loving an audience, I told the psychologist how the gap between the original spark of inspiration and the actual manifestation on the page, or in fabric, always depresses me. When I look at what I have written, the energy, the brilliance of the first idea seems to have thinned. Sometimes, as in the case of writing haiku, there is no gap at all. The 'Aha!' and the written lines are the same and I sigh with satisfaction. But this is a rare happening. The gap, I have now come to realize, occurs when my brilliant little brain steps in and my ego is written large on the page. Only when I step aside, disappear as it were, does the original creative flash and the words on the page seem as one.

I also told him how Eli struggles with his creative angel. Wrestling with the problem that he has, after all, set himself; being somehow his own angel and his own devil. Eli is willing to try the beginning of a sculpture nine, or ten times, Edison-style, until the pieces fall into place. In contrast, if my inspiration falters, I usually tear up the manuscript (I have been known to throw away whole books), or to extract a small section from it for a poem, before discarding the rest. When my fabric pieces lose their ties to their creative source, I undo them, or, in the case of knitting, usually find I can make a hat out of the wretched failure. My motto is: If it doesn't come easily, try something else. "Can one prepare for an 'Aha!' moment?" the psychologist asks, "Perhaps by becoming very still and focused?" I ponder this for a moment. I think how our modest home provides the stability and beauty that allows Eli and I to explore at will. But then I also think of a couple of wonderful poets I know who walk up and down in a room scattered with clothes on the floor and last night's supper on the table, producing wonderful verse. "You can hold yourself open," I reply, "but if you do it too intensely it will only lead to performance anxiety and a blank page."

I am carried away by my eloquence, when, on pausing for a breath, I notice that the psychologist has stopped asking questions or even giving me attention. He rubs his chin and looks carefully at Eli's pristine pieces. I wonder whether I have helped or hindered his research. I do notice that while he examines the joins and the structure of each sculpture closely, he is not even glancing towards the price label. This makes me realize that he is not about to explore them more closely in the warmth of his own home. Practical ideas such as this often intrude into my philosophical musings.

I felt depleted, and strangely annoyed. He must have sensed me turning away, for with profuse thanks he departed. I allowed myself to feel my emptiness and irritation at what was my apparent waste of time and words. Eli, much wiser than I, had merely greeted the psychologist and then disappeared into his workshop. He does not like to speak of his creative process, preferring the works to speak for themselves. But I, seduced by attention like a needy child, had allowed myself to be pumped dry. I decided to go out into the back garden and gather the branches broken off by a recent storm. "Maybe in my sweat, inspiration will strike," I thought. I am ever hopeful.

Recording this visit now, I wonder again what the psychologist, or I, had gained from the encounter. I suspect he will inevitably come up against that anonymous first source that leaves me scratching my head and not do any better with it than I have. Even if I look at the creative act from another angle, as my husband might – considering the exact math he needs to make his wooden spheres complete and his 'Moebius' Trip' (as one of one of his pieces is called) meet correctly – I am still confronted with the mysteries of measurement, proportions and equation which also fall in front of me like a misty but solid veil preventing further question.

Jean Erdman states that the way of the mystic and the way of the artist are related, except that the mystic doesn't have the craft. Hardly satisfying to my probes, or to the psychologist's, but perhaps where the matter has to be left for the moment.

Occasionally I have tried to express my exploration of the creative process in poetry as well as in essays. Here two poems attempt the seemingly impossible task of telling how writing comes into being.

Processing the News

She sat in her half acre
and received news on the radio
that a never-before played
trio by Enesco had been found.
And on TV she heard that
a dictator was about to overturn
another dictator and send
his Evil Empire packing.
Who's evil empire was not
quite clear and so the reverse
seemed as plausible to her.
Her email commanded her to sign
petitions to stop the dictators
doing what ever they were doing,
to rally against bullying in schools,
prevent clitoridectomy in Africa,
protest the treatment of women ...
Everywhere.
And a threat that if she didn't sign
a good luck letter she would
be cursed with bad luck.

Later, her neighbour brought her news
of a woman bitten by her friend's dog
and another woman by a stranger's
(dog that is), all in the same week
and on the same little bad dog island.
Her neighbour also told of some
poor folks who got an inheritance
and bought waterfront and some
rich folks who lost a packet on some deal
and had to move from waterfront
to some dirt track in the interior.
And 'Oh!" she said to some of this news,
and 'Aaah!,' she said to the rest.

In the evening, the book she was reading
informed her that 96% of the universe,
her universe, was made up of unknown stuff,
and that ten parts of her body could now
be replaced at a certain price,
and that she could be cloned in the very near future
if she should wish to be ... which she didn't,
already having a twin and finding that strange enough.

And as she lay in bed at night listening to JR country,
she learned that she should be sticking to the true values
of flag-waving and of small towns where the skyscrapers
are silos.

As she fell asleep she let the input of the day
swirl any way it might in her head ...
the oxymoron of honest politicians,
news of the sex-trade workers in Africa
and of AIDS there too, and of a starlet
who had been married three times and was barely twenty,
and of anti-ballistic missiles.

In the morning she got up and
reaching for her silk-covered journal,
she wrote:

snow still here
in the half-opened white crocus
a sleeping bee

Here another poet forces the creative act and not much
good will come of it, I can assure you.

Problems for a writer of light verse

He was away when
the hurricane hit the island,
likewise for the political scandal
about the trustees, and for the visit
of the choir from Soweto.
His present relationship
was causing him no pain,
and neither was his body.
Lacking angst he wandered
at a loose end along the beach.
He felt that there was not much to write
about in his rather dull life,
so he tried a haiku about seaweed

Perhaps Wallace Steven's confusing comments on his
poem "The Old Woman and the Statue" express the creative
process best for me:

"While there is nothing automatic about the poem, nevertheless it has an automatic aspect in the sense that it is what
I wanted it to be without knowing before it was written what
I wanted it to be, even though I knew before it was written
what I wanted to do."

As I now write of the psychologist's visit, I find myself having a minor 'Aha!' moment. I realize that just as a musician may be said to have been discovered over night, but usually has worked for years busking and in bars overlooked by one and all, the creative act that seems to come like a bolt from heaven is actually the result of hours of research. Of hours spent looking, probing, writing rubbish, making a stew of conversations overheard, books read, pictures seen, patterns broken, emotions disturbed. Of despairing, then writing more rubbish and wishing one was anywhere but at one's desk. The psychologist had, for some reason, leaned towards a mystical source for the creative act. I lean more towards the idea that the 'Aha!' moment is a tiny mushroom, its mycelium stretching acres underground, dependent on other soils, other climates, other donors. It has no one source.

Maybe now I will allow myself to stop wrestling with the question of what the origin of the creative act might be and just float on the magic carpet of trust, disciplining myself by reading and writing steadily, often without inspiration, yet somehow alert and ready to take action when inspiration does eventually come.

Ground Themes

There's nothing like fondness for a piece of home-turf to get one's creative juices flowing. I'm not just talking Walden here, nor Annie Dillard's beautiful Pulitzer Prize-winning book of nature writing – *Pilgrim at Tinker Creek*. This latter book has been critiqued and analyzed to death. Indeed, I just found a response journal that teachers can use with the book written by Brenda Walton, Ed.D. which can be found at www.teachersfirst.com/lessons/pilgrim/index.htm. American poet-laureate Billy Collins complains of his students wanting to tie poems to a chair and torture them and I am afraid that is what happens to beautiful poetic texts such as *Pilgrim at Tinker Creek*. Why can't we ever leave well enough alone?

Other books of the kind where the author visits a special place at regular intervals are *Watchers at the Pond* by Franklin Russell – a Canadian nature classic; the wonderful bird watching diaries of C. E. Tunnicliffe – *Shoreland's Summer Diary* and *Shoreland's Winter Diary;* that brilliant book where the author considers her own lawn for a year – *Surburban Safari* by Hannah Holmes; the English classic by Alison Uttley, *A Year in the Country;* and *There is a Season* where Canada's Patrick Lane weaves his backyard garden in with his memoirs in a real tour de force.

Walden, of course, conjures up the ideas of simple living and love of nature. I suspect it is seldom actually read these days. I was not surprised to learn recently that Thoreau's mother lived a couple of miles down the road from the pond, and I speculate, with a slight smile, that he wended his way there from time to time to get a shot of her home cooking. But then that just reflects my cynical nature that continually expects to, and often does, find a gap between idealists' thoughts and their actual lives.

Tunnicliffe's diaries were a basis for his later sketches and paintings. They are centred on his bird-watching and are clear, innocent and enchanting. *Suburban Safari* is a detailed observation, with emphasis on the biological processes, of the author's green parts of her garden. One of the chapters has a description of a storm that is as terrifying as any I have read. Alison Uttley drew on her farm-family home for much of her writing for adults and her clarity and keen observation make this book and *The Country Child* totally absorbing. When reading Uttley, we are there with her on her familiar ground. She was one of the first women to graduate in physics from the University of Manchester and her examination of the world around her is enchanting. Again I discovered, as with Thoreau, that there was a gap between the idyllic world she presented and the complications that her domineering per-sonality caused in her personal world.

Recently I came across a wonderful example of a book focused on 'place,' *The Path* by Chet Raymo. In this book an astronomy professor walked the same one-mile path for 40 years. Following it as it meandered from his home, through the woods, over a stream and through a meadow to the col-lege where he taught. Not only does he use this path as a base for essays on nature, but he also uses it to comment on the Industrial Revolution, geology, landscape architecture, astronomy and a host of other interesting topics. He urges his readers to walk attentively on whichever path they choose; stopping often to observe and listen with care.

I was attracted to this form of book and, as writers usually imitate the form that captivates them, I decided to adopt a nearby provincial park, Drumbeg Park, as my ground theme. When we first settled on Gabriola we visited the park, a ten-minute walk from our house, almost every day. Later, as Eli started his regime of swimming all year round in clement weather, we kept the visits to Drumbeg to those days when there was no rain, when the waves were not too high and when a sun, even if only weakly, managed to filter through the clouds.

Drumbeg Park is a small park, and not of any particular importance or attraction to visitors, there are no camping grounds or boat ramp. It does, however, have wild flowers, Garry Oaks, otters, seals and a variety of gulls and ducks; certainly enough for me to use the park for a series of essays, poems and sketches. In *Drumbeg Park,* I cover natural history, the park's history and the use of the park by the community. I even incorporated elements of the park into a fabric wall-piece after the book was published.

My exploration of haiku has made me more acutely aware of my surroundings – one has to be lazily alert to allow a haiku to pop through – and my move to Gabriola has made those surroundings both rural and seashore, plenty enough stimulus for nature writing. While I will never be good with details; I often confuse plants, am unable to distinguish gulls and cannot attach names to anything, yet still I have deep within a feeling that can make for strong poetry and thoughtful essays. The feeling is what the Japanese call *yūgen,* what Daisetz Suzuki calls 'The Unfathomable,' awe at the universe's immensity and mystery. Awe at the cycles and systems that imply a plan, but may very well be without one.

Here is a section from a chapter of Drumbeg Park. It is done in *haibun* form – a travel piece, interspersed with haiku.

Eagle-count

grey sky
and water also grey ... but
the eagle is back

The first week of January is eagle count time on Gabriola Island. We, though not birders, can readily identify mature and immature bald eagles and so we have been asked to count the eagles in Drumbeg Park.

It is dark when we rise and the fog still hangs steady as we put on layers of clothes, gather binoculars and walk along the gravel road to the park. As we come to the shoreline the fog starts to rise.

heavy fog rises
bay jammed with logs
and harlequins

But no eagles. We do know, however, that if we are early enough we will be able to count our one resident eagle on his tree. And, indeed, as we mount the crest of the park, there he is.

mist rising
eagle squatting on
his eagle tree

I mark 'one mature' in my notebook. This bird never fails to draw my admiration as he sits at the very top of the tree, eagle-eyeing all around him. He glances down momentarily as we pass, but dismisses us as non-prey and returns to gazing out over Breakwater and the other islands. Actually, he is a clumsy fisher, having to make many attempts before he emerges with a fish in mouth or claws. But so long as he stays on his tree, he appears to be emperor of Drumbeg.

The winter tides are high, so the shoreline is loaded with driftwood and logs from broken log booms. Locals gather them for fence posts and firewood – the latter at the peril of salt in the wood stove.

high winter tide
the waves braid over
the sandstone

We are having no luck in our count, but do stop to talk to two neighbours who are out early. We are immediately surrounded by a barking of dogs.

eagle count
two neighbours, three dogs
a flock of buffleheads

At the end of the park, before the houses of the summer residents, we halt. Raising our binoculars, we view the outer islands. On the closest, a small island belonging to a rather truculent gentleman, five otter are romping about. As this island has a "No Trespassing" sign on it, I am in awe of the otters' nerve.

five otter are romping
on the curmudgeon's island
how dare they!

I decided to self-publish *Drumbeg Park* since I thought it was only of local interest, and I didn't want to spend time going the rounds of publishers for what I thought was a pleasant, but not important, little book. Sometimes I get confused by my self-evaluation, thinking a minor manuscript major and vice versa. This modest little book has sold, and sold, and goes on selling. People tell me they are enchanted by its simplicity, its unpretentiousness, its sense of nostalgia for a time when all was innocence. Of course such a time never existed, but I often daydream of it as if it had. I used the park as a frame for a time that never was. I suspect that other writers of 'place' also use their chosen spot for whatever belief they have cobbled together to make their lives meaningful.

Unfolding Tales

In the beginning was the story. Well I suppose it was really 'the word' or perhaps 'the grunt.' Whichever it was, I am certain that when *homo sapiens sapiens* first started observing the movement of the stars and the cycles of plant growth, they started telling stories. Stories to explain what they were sensing, for humankind is a 'Why?' asking creature and those why's needed answers.

I think these explanations likely brought forth the first origin of the universe stories, which inevitably included a host of gods and goddesses projected in man's image. Along with the stories came moral rules, good triumphing over evil and, because people can only deal with so much horror without going mad, humour, which crept in at the follies of individuals and the stupidities of communities

These stories were likely told around fires on deep winter nights when both young and old gathered to hear them, for childhood, and childhood 'innocence' would not have been invented yet. It took Victorian prudery to 'clean up' these ancient tales, 20th century Disney to sweeten them, and the politically correct movement to ensure no one at all would be offended by any aspect of them, all of which rather destroyed their original purpose. I'm sorry but I still prefer 'woodsman' in *Red Riding Hood,* to the more correct 'wood-chopper person,' or, worse still, 'log-fuel technician.'

To this day, children, whatever some people might prefer to think, love gory details and subjects that hint of terror, just enough to thrill. Children have to be good to survive in a family, but they can't be good all the time; they are disobedient, they daydream, they answer back, conceal their thoughts and sometimes want to run away. This can give rise to guilty feelings. Children know they have a dark side that worries and sometimes threatens them. When they see it spelled out in stories, they come to realize that everyone shares this shadowside … it is part of the human condition. Folk tales become a safe place to explore our less than satisfactory aspects and, indeed, to realize we are all a mixture of good and bad. As G. K. Chesterton said, "Children already know about dragons. What fairy tales tell children is that dragons can be slain," or, I add, even befriended.

In spite of all this editing and rewriting, the storyteller has survived to this day and whether it's once upon a time, *mukashi, mukashi, il était une fois*, or *c'era una volta*, it is the signal for all activity to stop and for eyes to open wide as the storytellers unfold their tales. Using this captive audience, folktales, besides telling a good story, can inform on history, geography, or be a guide as to how we should react to each other and to the environment around us that nourishes us.

Bruno Bettelheim says of folktales, "The form and structure of fairy tales suggest images to the child by which he can structure his daydreams and with them give better direction to his life. More can be learned from folktales about the inner problems of human beings, and of the right solutions to their predicaments in any society than from any other types of story within a child's comprehension." Folktales nudge children towards adulthood in a less than perfect world.

While exploring folktales, I was interested to learn that the stories travelling by land change more than those carried by ships. As the story is told to one valley's people, they will adjust it to their ways of seeing and thinking before they toss it over the mountains into the next valley. By sea, it goes from one port to another almost unaltered.

In many ways the comic page in our newspapers is our modern form of storytelling. But here the heroes and heroines, the wise and foolish dogs and penguins, the villains and the plots involving them, all unfold at our breakfast table. Add to these miniseries of families and friends from "Dynasty" to "Six feet Under" and "Sex in the City," as well as sitcoms, and our folk-story-telling capacity is up and running. These modern folktales serve the same functions they did in previous times. They tell us our problems are universal problems, that every family has secrets and that we shouldn't fret so much about ours. They show us how others solve the problems we share, or live with life's uncertainties.

The detective genre is also a form of modern folktale where heroes undergo heroic journeys with many impediments before wrong is righted and the villain is destroyed, or at least in custody. I was very surprised to find that our local women's institute, which has a remarkable library, had true crime as one of its preferential purchases. Comics, TV miniseries and sleuth tales are our own stories told in our own way to make sense of a senseless world. Can it be possible that our folktales, which give meaning to our lives, are all about sex and violence? Or how to get our man or woman, and deal with the pressures at the office?

When retelling traditional stories, one approach is to use a modern vocabulary and settings so that the stories seem familiar and yet somehow still a little distant, or the stories can be retold in the traditional way, with more historically correct expressions. Either way, I think the important part of the retelling of folklore is to gain a deeper understanding of ourselves and the world we live in. In retelling one has to skirt the real danger of children adopting the cliché, the stereotype of say, mystics sitting in caves meditating as present day behaviour, when India has become a leading competitor in the computer world and is as fully part of the 21st century as North America.

I tried with my book, *Telling Tales on the Rim* to retell folk tales that had captured me and that for me had a moral, a lesson, of which I should take heed. I used the word 'telling' in three of its meanings – relating, having a force, or effect, and revealing something that otherwise might remain unnoticed. Children hate didactic stories where the moral hits them over the head, so I pushed the lessons to the back as far as I could and dwelt on the clash of good and bad, for children like to see things clearly delineated, since they never are in life. I also introduced the reader to origin stories, circular tales and added a few animal tales. I included stories of absurd happenings, the tall-tale liar and the 'simpletons' who just can't see the situation they are falling into, which the readers, can see so clearly and want to tell them to avoid. I wanted to offer a range of stories that not only showed examples of the available genre of folktales, but that would also engage a wide range of emotions. I finished up *Telling Tales on the Rim* with stories about the big questions that children start asking when they are three, and continue asking until they are 90 if they are at all wise.

When writing a modern folktale, there are certain rules that seem to apply. The storyline must be maintained – the predicament of the hero or heroine, the stumbling blocks made by the villain, the crisis and the solution. The storyline is the strength of the story, although the culture of the tale must be represented accurately. For the story, besides having a basic truth, is also about respecting other cultures. So here it is in a nutshell. First we have a familiar introduction then move quickly into action. Good should overcome bad, with lots of repetition, perhaps the heroine comes back the same way she went, with the same encounters, and a satisfactory conclusion. Maybe not always 'happily every after,' but at least 'live to see another day.'

I was writing *Images of Japan* in the days when Japanese culture had taken over my being, so I decided to insert a Japanese folktale of my own making. I had drifted so far into the Japanese culture that I even bowed to used car salesmen when making a purchase and subdued my opinions, only suggesting ideas as vaguely and unobtrusively as possible, in a gentle, 'female' voice. I imitated the Japanese-folk-tale form so successfully my story, *The First Kokeshi,* that I had teachers writing to me about how touched they were and how they had had to turn to the blackboard less their students should see their tears when the story was being read. I felt vaguely triumphant and terribly deceitful at the same time on receiving these comments.

Cultural appropriation is a very controversial matter these days. Some argue that First Nations should be the only ones to tell their stories and ask who can tell an African-American story better than an African American can, or, in my case, a Japanese folktale better than someone Japanese? I sit on the fence in this matter, as in most matters I am asked about. I muse that perhaps I was Japanese last lifetime and so possibly have a Japanese meme sitting perkily on one of my genes, which would make my writing of Japanese folk tales legitimate somehow. As they say every truth must have an opposite and equal truth to match, why not consider it?

My three favourite Japanese folk tales that I have retold, I called *The Enchanted Pool, One Straw Millionaire* and *Obasute Yama* (throw away old people mountain). The last title is the only one that is used in Japan, I believe. In *One Straw Millionaire,* a good, but penniless man, through faith and good deeds marries the warlord's daughter and acquires a fine horse. This dreaming of acquiring riches is a universal theme in folktales, but not one that appeals to me. When I hear myself saying "If only I had a million," I know it's time to get out in the garden to do some heavy weeding and come to my senses. Still, in *One Straw Millionaire* all the elements of a good folk story are there. Our hero's situation is hopeless. What can he possibly do? He appeals to a higher power and a series of adventures happen to him that gradually draw him, unsuspectingly, into good fortune. His virtues, plus his faith, make him triumphant.

As I age, the other two stories become more relevant. In *Obasute Yama* there is a time of famine in the village and the warlord commands all old people to be carried up the mountain and left there. One devoted child cannot bring himself to do this and so hides his grandmother in the cellar. The warlord is confronted by another warlord, who will invade unless three riddles are answered. Who answers them? Why, the boy's grandmother, of course. This is a great story for children, and adults, for North Americans already find themselves supporting a burgeoning number of seniors to whom they may not have positive feelings, perhaps considering them to be an unnecessary load rather than a source of wisdom. *The Enchanted Pool* deals with a situation that I used to find very witty, but as I age and Alzheimer-fears arise from time to time, the story has become less amusing and more a possibility.

Folktales are passed down in the mother's milk, through the mother's lullaby, the father's work song. They link us to our roots, and every child needs that rooting in order to move forward. And when the tale is told and eyelids are drooping, small ears may catch the moral embedded in the story and will definitely hear the promise that everything will turn out well in the end.

este cuento se ha acabado (Spanish)
e viveram felizes para sempre (Portuguese)
und sie lebten glücklich bis an ihr Leben sende (German)
ta men yi hou jiu kuai le de sheng huo xia qu (Chinese)

Owari – the end (Japanese)

Continue through the Middle

Pens, Pencils and a Yellow Pad of Paper

"How soon 'not now' becomes 'never.'" – Martin Luther

I'm not sure what Martin Luther was talking about specifically here, but for a writer guilty of procrastination (and which writer isn't?) the quote surely resonates. Over the years I have found my ways of procrastination have changed – at one time I used to pound the piano keys instead of the typewriter's, later I took to doing excessive housework, my favourite task being cleaning out the drawer where I stashed plastic and paper bags. These days, for delay, I've taken to gathering all my pens and pencils together from the various nooks where they have been scattered, almost as a miser would gather and count his gold. I lay them out on the dining-room table and then apportion them to the various rooms of the house where they can be at hand should inspiration arise. Before the allocation, however, it is my joy to go down to the basement, where a pencil sharpener is screwed to the wall, and sharpen all those bright yellow pencils. I do this ritual at least once a week.

Venus HB is my standard pencil. The traditional yellow painted stem cheers the darker corners of my dwelling. Occasionally I will use a propelling pencil (do they still call them that?) but, as I age, remembering to buy leads is just one more thing I am liable to forget. Pencils really only came into their own at the end of the 19th century when a French chemist, Nicolas Conte, fired a mixture of clay and graphite which he then put in a wooden case. The slit in the case that allowed this to happen was then sealed with a section of wood. With this process Conte could make the pencil 'lead' of varying degrees of hardness, and so H through HB to B was born. The UK manufacturers use numbers as well, so 9B is hopelessly smudgy and 9H so sharp it will pierce the paper. I tend to prefer the B end of the scale for love poems, and break endless 9H's when editing, particularly when editing other folk's work. Some American manufacturers use numbers to distinguish degrees of hardness, so if you are crossing the Atlantic, you need a little conversion table such as I use for knitting needle sizes (#1=B, #4=2H). There is no standard grading in the industry. You can read all about this in *The Pencil*, by Henry Petroski. As a final note, I have never found the little eraser at the end of the pencil to do anything but mess up the page, have you?

As far as the pen goes, I have used everything from quill (made from local seagull feathers) to fountain pen. I remember, somewhat fondly, from my school days, steel-nibbed pens and inkwells and the general mess that involved a stained index finger and blotting paper. For jotting down ideas I like a pen with free flowing ink to match the process. For editing hard copy, I find something a little dryer is needed. I love the sensualness of black ink on paper. I was for some years a student of shodō, Japanese calligraphy, where the enchantment of the shapes of the kanji and kana added to the enchantment of seeing black ink flow out on white rice paper. For some years I identified with the literary women of the Japanese court – Murasaki Shikibu and Sei Shonagon – and even wrote a reprimand to them that finished with my advice that they should get grinding that ink and start writing. The making of one's own ink is a wonderful centring process I find, but maybe those Japanese court ladies liked to procrastinate also.

Reprimand to those Japanese Court Women

Oh you stupid court women!
Have you nothing better to do
than spend long nights crying
into your futon about how
you can still feel his hands
in your dishevelled hair,
still smell the lingering scent
of his clothes on your own.
Why, anything triggers your tears:
the call of a mountain cuckoo,
the quail crying out,
or the plover piping.
Your buckwheat pillow is soggy
and your koto is out of tune.
Can't you see the paths
to your house are overgrown
and deep in snow.
You must understand that the gods
have decreed your north-westerly
direction forbidden to him
for the rest of the year
and probably the rest of your life!
Your heart may be withering,
the skies filled with clouds,
and even the moon is slow and sinking,
yet gazing at your soaked pillow,
and trying to unknot your twisted strands
will not help matters at all.
Why don't you read Sei Shonagon
and take matters into your own hands.
Start making lists, that will stop
the flow of your tears.
begin with 'Depressing Things'
and get them out of your system.
Next 'Things that Should be Short'
such as unrequited love.
Soon you'll be brushing your long hair
and grinding a load of fresh ink
in order to list
'Things that have lost their power.'

Nowadays I go for calligraphy brush pens and others that ooze a thick black line on to the page:

Something there is

Something there is
of ink on paper,
for, even as I write,
pulled to the contact point,
no longer conscious
of the words I am writing,
just the dark on light,
the something where
there was nothing ...
the pen tip, the ink,
the paper and I together
at one instant and all there
is, is flow.

I usually write my first ideas for a book on recycled bank statements, charity appeals and circulars. I gather these together and then put the second draft on the computer. Any editing is done from hard copy. There is something about my brain that prefers to look down, rather than look across. It seems it is sharper bowed in modesty.

The computer is not just valuable for research (although for this I occasionally call up a human reference librarian and find that he or she is often more reliable than Google, particularly when Google shows that 2,345,000 instances support one spelling and 2,200,000 support the opposite). Computers are also wonderful for gathering material into directories and files and shifting them around with abandon. The worst thing is that I often get lost in the maze of sub-directories I have for a book and can spend a whole morning editing the wrong file. Clear naming is the solution here. Proofreading is a cinch with a good spell-check and grammar program, though it is wise to decide ahead of time with your publisher as to which style book they are using. I use my own style book which sits on the 49th parallel between British and American spelling and punctuation. It drives my proofreader wild, but I'm a hybrid and that's that. The last word on computers for me is the thought of Dylan Thomas doing 60 rough drafts of his last poem without one; no wonder that finished him off.

Even though the computer allows me the aesthetically pleasing act of putting black words on a white screen with merely a key tap, the actual grasping of a pen, or pencil, gives me a bigger thrill when I write the very same words on paper. I'm not sure whether this is because I have the tactile pleasure of being in constant contact with the writing tool, having it under control as it were, or whether it is merely a memory, a memory trapped in my hand muscles, a precious memory of an earnest child caught in the wonder of seeing her thoughts materialize solid on her writing pad.

While writing this about my writing tools, my brain went off at a tangent, as it often does, and came up with the idea that not all procrastination is bad. To paraphrase Gertrude Stein, "I have only one set of hands, only one," so to procrastinate at housework, or cleaning the car is a good thing, for at least it gets a few chores done that need doing. However, making a to-do list and ticking the items off like fury is only fooling yourself that something is happening, unless all the items concern your writing life.

Writing that pushes you out of your comfort zone needs an extra little procrastination, that's understandable. I was zipping along carefree on a new book, when the manuscript for this book arrived ready for a giant overhaul. It may have been ready, but I wasn't. I froze rigid as a deer caught in the headlights, and only the kindly thought that my publisher might like to see a revised draft before she gave birth to her second child defrosted me enough to enable me to climb the stairs to my attic computer station. The threat of imminent labour (on her part) activated labour on mine one could say. Once writing, and way outside my comfort zone, I surprisingly enough found myself perfectly at home.

The Good, the Bad and the Point

I started writing for children because I wanted a new challenge and this one landed on my doorstep. Irrespective of a degree in social work, I have changed course at regular intervals throughout my life. I have been a market researcher, housewife, mother, statistical analyst, therapist, ESL teacher, photojournalist – none of these have been a wild success as a career, but all have been more than enough to carry me (somewhat bumpily) into the next one. Can one ask for more?

My ESL teaching career, which really steered me firmly into the writer's life, began in Japan. I went to Japan on a two-week holiday simply because I hadn't visited it before. My husband and I had decided to work it in (along with Hawaii) on the way to taking a trip on the Trans-Siberian railway. My first husband, who lived and worked in Japan, complained about our superficial travel behaviour. "Why don't you stay and get to know the country?" he asked. He, of course, had lived several years in Japan without even beginning to learn Japanese, but that is typical of folks giving this type of advice. But we took him seriously and, before he could protest, had both taken jobs as ESL teachers and had signed him up to sponsor us.

When we later returned to Canada for Expo '86 in Vancouver as photojournalists, we discovered that Japan had been put on the B.C. Ministry of Education's grade six curriculum. My husband and I decided that we probably knew more about Japan than most grade six students, and decided to stay in Vancouver. There we chose to further the grade sixes' knowledge of Japan by taking on yet another new career, this time as guest lecturers.

Along with visiting schools with a carload of kimono, geta, dolls and other Japanese items, we also showed slides. Our slides were entirely historical, and so gave a rather dated picture of Japan, as if samurai and their ladies were still around and the car industry hadn't yet been invented. The kids loved the ninja and armour shots and we were a great success. We decided to sell the Japanese slides in sets and found we needed to write accompanying notes. Thus, my life as a children's writer was born.

The slide kits led to the writing of other books on things Japanese. I started writing about Japanese folk toys, since I collected them, and used them as a hub on which to pivot a variety of facts in *Images of Japan*. I then added the retelling of folk stories to my writing output, and, as if there aren't enough good Japanese folktales, as I mentioned earlier, I added one I had written myself. I didn't see the need to mention this since the story was so close to traditional ones, and so I was amused when I got many a compliment from teachers on the touching Japanese tale.

I then wrote a book on the Japanese language and writing system, *Japanese – an appetizer*. I was hardly qualified for this, but did know, at that time, how to write the two syllabaries, katakana and hiragana, and 2000 of the Chinese letters that the Japanese had adopted, and adapted, via Korea, from the Chinese. It was an advantage being a fledgling at the language myself, for I understood what a beginner might need. The family that was going to have a Japanese student 'homestay,' or the child who was going to Japan on a boy scout exchange really just needed a few polite phrases and not too deep an understanding of sentence structure.

After that I took on an introduction to haiku for teens, *Haiku – one breath poetry*, a book that I still love, for it wrote me, as all the best books write their authors. It became something of a North American basic introduction to the subject, since it was an American Library Association Selection. It was, and still is, much given to children as prizes at cherry-blossom-writing-haiku-competitions.

Feeling fairly confident about writing for children by now, I switched to subjects other than those Japanese and wrote a book about names, a book on imagination and a couple of crossword and word-game books. I even took on a book about Chinese inventions, although I had never visited China. Still, I was interested in the subject and learned that you do not need to be exhaustively knowledgeable about a topic, as long as you checks your facts thoroughly and don't write down to the child.

As far as fiction goes, I have only done one title for children, *One Day a Stranger Came*. It came to me fully written in a dream and I wrote it down and submitted it with the sleep still on my eyelids. Months went by without news. I finally decided to call the publishers – a forbidden thing to do. They were surprisingly pleased to hear from me. They had sent my manuscript to reader and it had got lost. "Lost!" I cried in great dramatic form, and with lots of indignation put into that one little word. They quickly asked me to resubmit, and whether it was from guilt that they had mislaid my manuscript, or whether the story was actually good enough to print, print it they did. But before the printing came the editing with the title changed and various aspects of the story modified. It was my first title with a large publisher and so I acceded to all their wishes.

Alison Uttley, the English writer who wrote many books for children, laid out the following principles for guiding her writing in children's books. She demanded truth in the background to serve as a solid foundation for even a thistledown tale. She required that each story should have a legend, a proverb, or a scrap of wisdom in it, and that the story should have an implicit morality. She also felt that children's stories should allow them to feel safe, with good prevailing over evil, and with the inclusion of only small fears that could be surmounted.

Having only written one juvenile fiction, I couldn't possibly trap all those qualities in 32 pages, could I? Now, retelling of folktales, of which I've done somewhat more, allows morality to come in by the bucket, for almost every tale warns of the results of bad behaviour, or tells the rewards of being good.

In the years I have written for children, I have gathered together things I need to do when I write for them as well as the things I definitely do not need to do. Having advice, of course I must share it, so here goes:

- When writing non-fiction, choose a topic you know well and are interested in, or a topic that you know nothing about, but would like to know something about. In either case, your enthusiasm and energy will be there for your young reader.

- Children have limited experience, so make the facts, in either your fiction or non-fiction, relevant to their home turf e.g., if doing a book on the earth, describe size and quantity by using hamburgers, sugar cubes, body parts, baseball scores.

- Keep the young reader right in the middle of your subject by addressing them directly for example., "If you were paddling down the Amazon ..."

- Don't waste your adjectives – nice, lovely and big don't say much. If you must use those words, use metaphor to show as big as, as nice as, or, as lovely as.

- In non-fiction, involve the children physically – introduce activities that will get them moving, or thinking of moving such as, "A chemist mixes his chemicals carefully like your mom measures and mixes the ingredients for those chocolate chip cookies you like so much."

- Children (and adults) like 'Wows' so point out extreme aspects of your subject to catch the reader, then fill in the possibly less-exciting details. Good photographs and attractive charts really help. For the present generation of children it is the picture rather than the word that has impact.

- Check your facts accurately, with specialists if need be; they are generous with their time.

- Don't talk down to children, chat directly. Whether you are writing fiction or non-fiction, if there is nothing between you and what you want to tell the child, your integrity will win them over.

- Don't tell the young reader more than they want to know, just because you are caught up in the subject. Children prefer small bits of information and this preference has been exaggerated by the sound-bites they are fed these days by the media they use.

- Get children thinking, analysing and querying. As a child I endlessly questioned teachers in order to distract them, however I only fooled myself, for that questioning has become entrenched as part of my way of life, as I hope it will become for all your young readers.

- If you are writing for nine-year old children, contact the nine-year old child inside you and you can't go wrong.

Once you have written for children, you often encounter the sticky subject of censorship. I once wrote an article on censorship for librarians and teachers during the days of Pacific-Rim Publishers, when my husband and I published and distributed supportive multicultural educational material, that I would like to share with you. After that I'll approach the subject of censorship less amusingly, as it is a worrisome area for children's writers.

Thoughts on the Human Body, on a Rainy Vancouver Day.

I am looking at a picture of Botticelli's "Birth of Venus" and am appalled to see what ugly ankles and feet she has; totally mismatching the slender body above. The reason that I am looking at her so intently, is that I am comparing her body with a nude in a book of Korean folktales for children. Both figures have hair cascading down and discretely covering vital areas. The Korean illustration does rather better in the area of modesty than the Botticelli, since the latter leaves one breast totally exposed. The reason that I am comparing the two nudes is that the Korean folktale book has just been rejected by a provincial Ministry of Education because of the said "nude on page 16."

I should mention that there are seven other water nymphs in the picture on page 16, most of them are well under the water with just the odd outline of a breast. I am perplexed as to why students can look at the "Birth of Venus" and yet not the water nymphs. Were it on ground of artistic merit, I would agree immediately, but I think that that is not the concern of the "reader" who rejected the book. I think the concern was to protect children from knowing how women look like without clothes on, and that surprises me, since any self-respecting child that I know will have that knowledge long before kindergarten.

I am musing on the situation when I suddenly remember that I have just added to our catalogue the story of a little Japanese boy who goes to the public baths with his grandfather. I reach out to take this new book from the shelf and give it a closer look. Yes, no doubt about it, Japanese subtle-illustration style or not, there are two instances where unmistakable male sexual organs can be seen, albeit roughly sketched. I muse more deeply.

The story is of a little boy who worries that his grandfather is lonely living on his own. He visits his grandfather and together they go to the public baths, stopping on the way to talk to all the many storekeepers who are his grandfather's friends. At the baths, as the steam rises from the blistering water, all is warmth and gossipy, neighbourly friendship. The little boy realizes that grandfather is not lonely after all. I close the book (penises and all) and feel very happy that such a wonderful little story exists and that I have it in our catalogue.

Being a writer and publisher these days is not easy. Writing this piece on a rainy day in Vancouver, I feel life is a slow series of shattered illusions. Illusions are what keep us going, and they shouldn't shatter too fast. I also nurse illusions from time to time, such as the one that librarians sit at polished desks, leafing through the latest glossy catalogues and choosing what ever their hearts desire. Librarians, too, are subject to the same human foible; as I talk to them at conferences and library meetings they often say to me, "How wonderful, you spend all day writing."

I join them in a misty vision of the Edwardian lady sitting at her roll-top desk and gazing out into the bouquet-splendid English garden, while a kitten plays at her feet. In my case the truth is rather cruder. From one of the windows in my third floor eyrie workroom, I see a tangle of hydro wires and the occasional smiling face of a Hydro man, who seems to come weekly to string up more. From the other window, two dumpsters invite a stream of street people searching for lost dreams.

My desk is laden with books, papers and dust, so that when I sneeze, the dust rises in little streams only to resettle in a comfier position on some other books or papers. I am pounding on the keyboard with my right hand, in a politically correct manner, while my left hand urgently searches for the delete key to offer some critical thinking to accepted assumptions. My left big toe taps the floor lightly trying to remember myself as a seven-year-old child who once opened her arms to the wide, wonderful, mysterious world, while the smaller toes on the left foot chatter among themselves as to whether Botticelli shouldn't have had Venus' hair cover both breasts and perhaps have let a long wayward lock descend to conceal those wretched ankles.

"But your right foot?" you will ask, "surely your right foot is doing something unfettered and creative and just what we need to support the grade six curriculum. Tell us what your right foot is doing?" All I can do is bow in deep Japanese apology over my keyboard and confess to you that my right foot … well, my right foot happens to be firmly pressed against the door keeping the wolf out.

Now for a slightly deeper look at censorship. As E. P. Morgan said, "A book is the only place where you can … explore an explosive idea without fear that it will go off in your face." Children should feel safe to explore in what they read. The question is how far should they explore, and it is here that censorship steps in. A book written for an adult

audience may not be suitable for a bright ten-year-old child ...
but why not? The child can understand the words and probably most of the concepts, why do we feel reluctant then to let
them read what is out there? Librarians talk about a 'normal
range of development,' but that is such a tenuous thing to
decide. How do we decide what to include in our writing for
children? Is every subject appropriate for the young?

There are trivial complaints made to librarians by parents,
which I feel can be quickly discarded, such as the fact that a
bottle of wine was in Red Riding Hood's basket for her granny,
(are beer commercials banned?) or the fact that a black rabbit
and a white rabbit get married in another book! But then we
come to a greyer area. When should children know the names
for the sexual parts of the body (as distinct from the non-sex-
ual)? Since children already know slang words from their
school-yard information bank, why not let them know the
real names, which don't have such a degrading sound. The
furore over Robie H. Harris' book *It's Perfectly Normal* seems
perfectly stupid to me, and the removal of Roger Pares *The
Annick ABC* because "N is for nudist eating noodles in Naples"
is just laughable. This book, I find, is not in my Vancouver
Island Regional Library system, so I can only imagine how
witty this picture page is.

Books that promote racism, are homophobic, or idealize
criminal behaviour are obviously out at all levels of reading,
at least for me, but the child should also learn that people are
racist, homophobic and criminal. When is a child ready to
learn that this is the way the world is?

Teachers and parents yearn for children to get off the
computer and their cellphones and read. When the Harry
Potter series came along the children did just that, with bells
on, even poor readers struggled through 400 page books. Yet
the series became probably the most censored one in the his-

tory of children's literature. *Forever* by Judy Blume is not far behind when it comes to censorship, as is that beautiful book by the great children's writer, Katherine Paterson, *Bridge to Terabithia*. Why? Because the author uses the words hell and damn and one of the characters is a non-believer! By the way, Judy Blume tells of an occasion when someone called her on the phone and asked if she was the author of *Are you There God? It's Me Margaret*. Blume said she was and the caller yelled, "Communist!" then slammed the phone down. A bemused Blume couldn't figure out whether the caller had equated Communism with menstruation, or religion, the two concerns in Margaret's life.

As textbooks and general reading in schools are taken over by mammoth firms such as Scholastic and McGraw-Hill Ryerson, firms that seem to me to want to avoid controversy at all costs, how are children to learn about the many views and approaches that come from living in a pluralistic society? Family values, religious and political beliefs vary wildly. Is there room for all of them without treading on toes? How about just respecting the child's right to read? Luckily book-banners don't know anything about marketing, for the sales of a banned book always shoot up when the ban is generally known.

Censorship is at its worst when publishers and writers begin to listen to the censor sitting on their shoulder. Education means "to lead out" to help the child explore the universe. Letting a small group of extreme-opinioned censors influence the general public is unforgivable.

Children love to be scared (not too much), they love to know what it is adults don't want them to know, they love books where the kid is disobedient to his or her parents, or runs away from home, or when the book contains bathroom humour. Children also love to laugh and parents are even getting paranoid about books that make their children happy! Because children love these edgy topics doesn't mean that reading books covering these topics is going to turn a child into a raving criminal, or a street child. In many countries, such as Japan and Denmark, sex and nudity are a natural part of life and are portrayed as such in their literature. So why shouldn't children enjoy stories of how a young couple in love make a baby, or how a little boy goes with his grandfather to the public baths?

The American Library Association states that more than one book a day faces expulsion from free and open public access in U.S. schools and libraries every year. Fear seems to be the basis for parental calls for censorship. Of course, all parents are afraid that their child will have bad experiences and come under the influence of harmful people, that's natural. What is not natural is the fear parents have that they are losing control over their child and that the child will start to think for itself and may, perhaps, question the style of life that the parents propound. A child has the right to explore who they are and how they can fit usefully into the world around them. Book censorship does not help.

Please don't let all the above make you fearful about starting to write for children. You can't hold back if you have a good story to tell and you must trust that most publishers won't censor it, and that most school boards won't remove it. Or why not be like Jim Trelease, who when writing on just this subject of censorship, told how he has a daily prayer that someone will ban one of his books so that he could see it leap up the charts.

As a postscript on censorship, I recommend "Capital "T" Spells Trouble. Ten "Dangerous" Books and why teens need them" an article on the web by Cathy Belben.

It's all Words and Games

As a child, I played endless word games with my twin sister, Ruth. I somehow assumed that my mother had given birth to her at the same time as me in order to provide me with a playmate and a wordmate. My parents, each a child of immigrant parents who were never able to master the English language, valued books and the spoken word highly. My father's reading focused on spy and war stories, the First World War being his time of greatest aliveness, which I suppose it was for many who found themselves surrounded by death on the battlefield. My mother favoured novels with a social protest theme – John Galsworthy and Karel Čapek come to mind; also John Betjeman, whose poetic style she adopted when she started to write poetry later in life. It was my two half-sisters who were the most earnest readers in our household and their Left Book Club books filled the bookcases. Mr. Gollanz had bravely started this publishing wing to counteract the growing threat of Fascism. It is to Effie and Betty Planker that I owe my lifetime love of words and my endless childhood days playing word games to which they introduced my twin and I. In such an atmosphere it is not surprising that I grew up to become a writer, and Ruth, who also has a few books under her belt, to become a Scrabble whiz.

When Ruth visited our little island a summer or two ago, a habit of hers reminded me of those childhood years. My twin has a short attention span, and if she is left alone too long she reads everything she can get her hands on, including the instructions for the fridge if she can't find anything else handy. During one of these restless periods, I heard her voice calling up the stairs "Give me a long word." I paused, then quickly my mind shifted into gear, "Christmas," I called down remembering that was one of our favourite words for a word game in which one had to find the maximum number of words one could make out of the given letters. "Too easy!" came her response and, once again, I remembered that, yes, it was too easy. "Extricate" I tried again. "Fine." she responded and was quiet for a few minutes. She then climbed the stairs triumphant with the 30 words she has extricated from extricate.

As I age I seem to incorporate my childhood habits into my writing, so I was not surprised to hear myself promise an educational publisher that I would produce a book of word games in the space of three months. Having made the promise, I rushed home, cast myself into a childhood mode and started to remember all the word games of my youth.

Words from a word, as I described above, was one of my favourites, but I also loved anagrams. An early apocryphal one was attributed to Pilate, who asked Jesus *"Quid est veritas?"* (What is truth?) Jesus replied in anagram *"Est vir qui adest"* (very roughly translated as "It is the man who stands before you") but, of course, it would have all been in Aramaic wouldn't it?

And then there was the word game involving morphing, although the word 'morphing' probably didn't even exist when I was changing 'dog' into 'cat' and 'boy' into 'man' in three moves, changing one letter at a time. Nowadays I wrestle with five letter morphs such as, 'bride' to 'groom' in eight moves. Inventing words for situations and things that didn't seem to have words that matched them was another fun thing to do when we were young, and I still hear occasionally on a radio program someone asking for a word to describe ... "days when you don't know what to wear," or a word for "the top of your feet." Well, I'm sure there's a medical word available for that place, but none in common usage.

Ruth and I used to enjoy inventing acrostics, where the first letter of a number of words spelled a description of what all the words had in common. Here is an example of an anonymous calendar acrostic:

JANet was quite ill one day
FEBrile trouble came her way.
MARtyr-like, she lay in bed;
APRoned nurses softly sped.
MAYbe, said the leech judicial
JUNket would be beneficial.
JULeps, too, though freely tried,
AUGured ill, for Janet died.
SEPulchre was sadly made.
OCTaves pealed and prayers were said.
NOVices with ma'y a tear
DECorated Janet's bier.

I've tried to find the source for this, but haven't located it. It has a strangely Victorian ring to it, and is really not the easiest way to remember the months. Groucho Marx's favourite poem, "Thirty days hath September" certainly provides more information. As one ages, I find that mnemonics prove less helpful for the remembering of things, since it is often the mnemonic itself that cannot be recalled.

Another of our favourite word games was "fruit, flower, fish and vegetable." I believe it is called Categories in North America. In this game, my twin and I would choose the categories and list them down the side of the page – fruit, flower, fish, vegetable, body of water, girl's name, etc. Then we would open a book at random and choose the first word on the page whose letters were all different. We would then write that word across the top of the page, each letter heading its own column. The game then was to try and find a word in each of the categories listed at the left that began with the letter at the top of the column.

A Rebus is a puzzle which uses pictures to represent words, or part of words and no self-respecting comic book of my childhood would be without a full-page story done in rebus format. Ruth and I, of course, could decode them in a flash. The rebus, I suppose, originated from coats of arms, where the owner's name was often alluded to in pun form. Recently I saw the coat of arms of the late queen mother. It had, among other things, quarters that were stylized lions and bows (archery.) This was a pun on her family name of Bowes-Lyon. The rebus, a strangely dated game, has now re-emerged in the advertising world, showing up in slogans such as, "I (picture of a heart) NY," and to some extent in the abbreviations used in email correspondence. Suddenly my father comes into my word-game picture with rebuses, for I have recalled one he wrote for us to decipher:

If the B MT, put more : if the B . putting more :

(If the grate be empty, put more coal on. If the grate be full, stop putting more coal on.)

Ouch! But how we loved it when we were children.

Hangman, a frequent game both at home and at school, is now in video game form (as, of course, is Scrabble, the most successful word game of all.) In case you don't know hang-man, a gruesome, politically incorrect gallows is drawn on a page with a series of dashes under it representing letters in the word to be guessed. As the guesser fails with a letter, a piece of the hanged man is drawn on the gallows. The aim is, of course, to guess the word before your completed man gets hanged. I can still hear Ruth calling out, "Give me an 'e'" and myself replying, "Yes, on the 4th," (the 4th letter is an 'e').

My twin just reminded me of the hours we played Lexicon, a precursor to Scrabble, apparently still available, and still with a following. In Lexicon the cards, each with a letter on it, are dealt out and the players vie with each other in getting words from the hands they have been dealt and getting their cards out first.

Word squares were another game of ours. They have been around since the Greeks used them on monuments, but the 19th century saw their peak of popularity. Word squares usually contained words of equal length that can be read both vertically and horizontally. Ruth and I never got beyond inventing four-letter word squares – squares in which each word occurs twice e.g.

```
C A S E
A C I D
S I N G
E D G E
```

More literate folk can produce seven-letter word squares, although if you are reaching for eight, or nine-letter word squares you are really going to have to incorporate the unusual and obscure. Tony Augarde challenges you in his *Oxford Guide to Word Games*, by saying, "the world is wide-open for someone (or some computer) to construct a really acceptable ten-word square." So off you go! Ruth and I made word squares into a game by calling letters out alternately and fitting them into a five by five grid best as we could, to see how many words we could make so that, if one line finished up 'beard' we could score 'be,' 'bear' and 'ear,' as well as 'beard.' In later word square development clues were added to the word square to help people guess the word and from that it was just a hop, skip and jump to the crossword.

Having put the cart before the horse, I should mention, that riddles were by many years the first word games. My father would bombard us with such corn as, "What is white and black and red all over?" (a newspaper) and a slightly exciting one to our young ears, "What did the needle say to the thread in the nudist colony?" ("So what?") As I write this I wonder whether this riddle didn't lead to Ruth, years later, deciding to holiday at nudist camps. The lesson to be learned from this riddle is that one should constantly be aware of the terrible (or marvellous) influence you can have on a child by using an unusual word.

The most famous riddler was, of course, the Sphinx, who hung around outside Thebes accosting travellers with the following riddle: "What goes on four legs in the morning, on two legs at noon, and on three in the evening?" If you didn't give the Sphinx the right answer, you died. Oedipus came along and did provide the correct answer, and the Sphinx had to kill itself as it had promised. Oedipus, though triumphant for the moment, didn't finish up too well himself. A lesson perhaps, in regards to hubris. As we have been through at least two of the phases described in the riddle, we know immediately that the answer is "man." I'm pleased to add that the idea of the Oedipus complex is now out of fashion and the forecast is that we all have a good chance of reaching the "three-legged evening," or rather the six-legged, (us + walker).

Of course, I mentioned some of these games I've just described in my book *Word Challenge,* and I also added games built around palindromes, lipograms, rhopalics and other such entities, (no, you look them up, or, better still, buy the book). Well, I'll relent and at least tell you that a lipogram is "the oldest artifice in western literature," according to a Mr. Perec. He wrote a whole novel called, *A Void* without using the letter 'e,' to create a lipogram, which is a body of writing that excludes one letter. This, in turn, reminds me of a brilliant story performed by Corey Frost at one of Gabriola's famous poetry events. The story he read was about what happens to the world when the letter 'q' is retired.

After I had spent a happy three months meandering and reminiscing, as above, and had finished editing the book, I glanced at Google where I found 8,000,000 entries under the words 'word games.' I'm glad folks are still playing with words, although I cannot imagine two children, such as Ruth and myself, now giving quite so many hours to them, unless they were played on a computer. The present youth generation is far more visually-oriented, I think, and put their energy into eye-hand coordinating video games, rather than the mind-searching skills needed in word games. This is great if you are going to become a surgeon, but not so applicable if writing is going to be your means of expression and income. Of course, starting with word games it was natural for my twin and I to move into Scrabble and crosswords as we aged. Which brings me to the time I wrote some crossword books.

Writers read. Apparently the more they read, the better their writing becomes (or so I'm told). Or, more likely, they give up writing all together, reckoning, as Will Rogers said, "it is easier to go out and buy a book than write one." I wonder whether writers also do more crossword puzzles than ordinary folks. Puzzle solving, it has been suggested, may be an archaic remnant of a survival strategy. Crosswords do have their own little niche when it comes to surviving in a crazy world, but their actual roots are not so ancient.

The first crossword appeared in the *New York World* in 1913 and it is Arthur Wynne we have to commend (or blame) for this invention that has absorbed hours of our leisure (and not so leisure) time. Crosswords began to appear frequently after it was discovered by publishers that folks would buy endless crossword books to fill their idle hours and that it wasn't too expensive to find clever folk to construct them.

I am not a cruciverbalist (crossword aficionado) but I have published two crossword books in my time, both of them put together in a lengthy, ponderous, studious kind of way and both enormously fun to do. These puzzle books weren't particularly easy, nor were they as difficult as say advanced cryptic crosswords are. They were for students, and each crossword was themed. The first book was based on countries around the Pacific-Rim and the second, on provinces across Canada.

Simple, you'll say, there is just the grid, the fill and the cluing. You get a pile of travel books and run through them looking for suitable words. You make a list of them, and then you build the crossword around them. Well yes, that's exactly what I did, but it wasn't that simple. As all crossword inventors know, there is the creator and then the editor. I never failed to plan a crossword that didn't, on fine inspection, have a misspelled word, a missing number for a word (so all the numbers had to be adjusted), or an impasse where I had to dance a tarantella to find a space for a 'perfect' word I wanted to use. In newspapers, it is the crossword editor who has to bear the brunt of angry letters when a mistake occurs in a printed puzzle.

Nowadays, there is software you can buy to make crosswords. But, of course, as someone who won't even use a sewing machine, preferring hand-sewing, I always choose the Luddite way, and so created the crosswords myself, although my husband did make a macro that helped me insert the black squares when I needed to. Recently I have read that even New York Times crossword constructors prefer not to use computer-prepared grids and definitely do not use suggested wordfill and clues.

The best crosswords, unlike the ones in my books, are symmetrical, don't have two-letter words, and should have half as many black squares as white, showing the cleverness of the constructor at interlocking words. Mine tended towards the American crossword puzzle which is information-based since that was the aim of the two books. English puzzles depend much more on wordplay and strategies – anagrams, puns and cryptic clues. American puzzles tend to have far more interlocking words, where solving one word can help the solving of others, and each letter is often connected to at least two others. British puzzles are cleverer and are harder to solve, while American puzzles are harder to construct.

Crosswords have supporters and attackers. H. P. Lovecraft complained "In a way crosswords do harm by cluttering up the mind with an aimless heap of unusual words selected for purely mechanical exigencies and having no well-proportioned relation to the needs of graceful discourse." Indeed, while one can learn some facts by using a reference source to complete a puzzle, often the clue is a direct translation and one does not learn anything particularly new about 'striding' when answering the clue "taking large steps." Then there is the colossal waste of time … one web blogger reckoned six days of a year, not perhaps as bad as TV or computer-game occupied time, but definitely a chunk. Perhaps this negative feeling about the educational possibilities of doing crosswords is best stated in the opinion that the best thing you get out of doing crosswords is getting better at doing crosswords.

To counter this rather jaundiced view of crosswords, medical evidence lists them, along with other mental activities, as able to ward off, or at least slow down, the oncoming of Alzheimer's disease. Lewis Kaplan from Alzheimer's Australia, supports this view and claims that people who do crosswords are less likely to move towards dementia. Certainly a strong associative memory, a large vocabulary and strength in the seeing of patterns and connections are requirements for successful crossword doers and these are good things to have. Intelligence is often defined as the art of making connections, so intelligence and crossword playing do seem to have a close relationship. To paraphrase Marc Romano, in order to do crosswords successfully, you need to become a highly organized collector of data about the world around you in an associative way. Another healing aspect of crosswords is the ritual of doing the crossword every morning over breakfast. This practice goes along with other rituals that reduce stress levels.

The ability to do crosswords certainly indicates mental agility and smarts. Crosswords also provide a diversion from daily worries; a diversion from which one might be able to return to reality with perhaps fresh solutions. Of course crosswords can produce their own pile of frustrations if a person isn't skilled enough to finish one. Will Shortz, the editor of the New York Time's crosswords, feels that people who do crosswords know a lot about the world and have to focus that knowledge, and this, he feels, makes for better people. Indeed Marc Romano in his book, *Crossworld*, remarks again and again on how good-natured, honest and decent the 500 or more attendees at the American Crossword Puzzle Tournament were. As I mentioned above, people with a wide range of general knowledge (preferable to the slightly derogatory word "trivia") often are good crossword folks and Romano echoed this idea at the 2004 American Crossword Puzzle tournament, saying that "people who have a tremendous body of general knowledge about the world tend to be a little bit kinder."

Romano perhaps waxes more eloquent than most on the values of a good crossword: "The grid is aesthetic … because the frequency and placement of black squares versus white make up the difference between an elegant and an inelegant puzzle; the fill is ethical because it has to adhere absolutely to certain practical rules; the cluing is a puzzle's metaphysics, since it represents the interface between the puzzle and its potential solvers – the means by which disorder of non-solution is transformed into the order of one complete and correct solution."

Crosswords often demand a knowledge of popular culture of which, I, as a TV-less, non-movie-going poet have a marked lack of. They are very 'of the moment' and I'm afraid I, in spite of my occasional haiku-writing, am not. One of the redeeming features of crosswords are that they give one the excuse to collect dictionaries and pass the time perusing the same, for irrespective of the immediate response I can get from Google for the name of a river in Auvergne, or a temple in Bali, I prefer to wade through dictionaries allowing myself to wander off, following up distractions. There's nothing like the rustle of onion skin pages to sooth the heart.

I adapted my puzzle books for educational publishers by adding lists of books for each puzzle that the students might read while searching for clues, thus, while completing the puzzle the student will also have read widely on the particular topic. In everyday crossword doing this is often frowned upon; one perhaps should weigh up for oneself the satisfaction of filling the crossword against the dissatisfaction of being left with the mild feeling that one has slightly "cheated." But to me the satisfaction of filling letters into squares doesn't need any other justification as long as the brain is being stretched.

The difficulty of the puzzle, of course, often depends on the difficulty of the clues, which can bring you to an impasse so that, with only a few clues solved, you toss the paper aside in disgust and go away. Yet you find that when you return to the puzzle latter (for you can't resist) some clues have become totally clear and you wonder why you couldn't have found the answers in the first place. This technique of walking away from a problem and turning to other interests is, of course, a basic problem-solving technique, not just a crosswords-solving technique.

Both the making of crossword puzzles and the solving of them are things of great delight to me, although my hubris doesn't go so far as solving them in pen, like my twin probably does. David Sedaris in his essay "21 Down" expresses how devastated he felt when he lighted on his friend doing the Friday New York Times with a ballpoint pen. Sedaris, in this brilliant essay, expounds that beginning to do crosswords in middle age is a way "to stave off the terrible loneliness." Ambrose Bierce, that great definer of words, used the doing of the New York Times Crossword puzzle with a pen as a definition for "Egotism." The New York Times' crossword, in case you don't know, grows harder with the days of the week. Monday is for the beginner and Saturday's is impossible.

Coral Amende, in *The Crossword Obsession,* praises the doing of crosswords for being "one of the ways in which we have created harmony out of chaos and brought some small semblance of order, however transitory or illusional, to our lives." But then we created the mess in the first place, didn't we?

Echoing Coral Amende's positive comments, I would like to finish with Marc Romano's touching advice when watching someone doing a crossword puzzle: "Whatever you do, don't disturb that person – he or she is solving a mystery and at the same time putting back together, word by word, the pieces of our broken world."

Sudoko seems to be sweeping crosswords to one side when it comes to wasting time. However, they call on the deductive parts of the brain and do not really compete in any way with the folk who prefer inductive thinking and are trivia driven. People will waste time no matter what, is my general view.

Interesting web-sites and links:

- Facts on the New York Time's Crosswords and their creators: http://home.everestkc.net/nytxword

  This site claims to have links to all known crossword-related sites and also supplies information for crossword generating

- "One Across" by Daniel Cappello (*The New Yorker,* March 4th, 2002) has numerous interesting references, probably more than you will ever need.

Don't Quote Me

Some years ago I was diagnosed with cancer. In a wild panic, I turned to meditation, macrobiotic diet and aromatherapy. I devoured a slew of uplifting and encouraging books on the subject, mostly of the genre "how to survive a cancer episode with a stiff upper lip and at the same time have it smiling." I read Deepak Chopra, Susan Weed, Karen Gelmon, Susan Love, John Link, Steve Austin and Cathy Hitchcock. Their books piled up on the coffee table. My worried husband downloaded stacks of articles from the web and I ploughed through them all. Occasionally I would read something that seemed apropos, something that lifted my heart, that even made me smile, and those things I wrote down. Before I knew it, the sheets of useful quotations that I had extracted had collected into a book-size manuscript.

One day a publisher came to consult me about some book she was thinking of publishing. She noticed the pile of papers that had my healing quotes on them, and, while I made a snack, she idly flipped through them. Before lunch was over she had insisted on printing the quotations as a book. A publisher behaving in this way is a rare happening, and I didn't argue with her on her decision. That is how *Healing Bag* came to be. It didn't cure me, and I doubt it cured anyone else, but it did change how people who read the book behaved towards their illness, for I got many letters telling me so. Long after it was published, an islander came up to me at some island potluck and told me how she and her husband had read from *Healing Bag* every day during his last months, and how reading and discussing the wise quotes I had gathered helped prepare him for his journey, and her for her loss. As often happens at island gatherings, where bad times and good times are shared in community, we fell into each other's arms weeping.

Although I didn't do another quote book for Lightsmith Publishing, the publisher of *Healing Bag,* I did publish two other books with them, one on writing your memoirs and one on haiku. However, the quotation bug had caught me and I went on to help produce a series of eight quotation books. It happened this way.

My twin, Ruth Artmonsky, she of Scrabble-playing fame, lives in London, England. I live on the small island of Gabriola, in the Georgia Strait. We are not quite at opposite sides of the globe, but, to all intents and purposes we might as well be. She lives in the middle of London, in Covent Garden, in a million dollar apartment. I live in a tiny, vinyl-sided cottage at the sparsely-populated end of a small island, where six cars past the house in one day is heavy traffic. She is wealthy, while I am living on a poet's income. She wears designer clothes … well I do too, if I can find them at Value Village. In spite of these material differences, we share a love of books, art and music. Occasionally Ruth flies over to our island, which she once described as "that scrub island in the Pacific" and, seemingly scared of trees, prefers to sit around playing Scrabble and piano duets during her visits. At the time of the particular visit about which I am going to tell you, I had just had my book of quotations, *Healing Bag,* published.

Ruth had brought with her a strange gift. It was two small books of quotations that we had apparently been given (so the Ex Libris stated) by an Aunt and Uncle when we were young girls, 60 years before. The little books brought back memories of how I used to love quotations and how I had profusely punctuated my school essays with them, making sure the best and strongest were kept for the beginning and for the end.

During my twin's visit, she read *Healing Bag* and looked at a new collection of quotes I had gathered on art; a subject about which we both knew a fair bit. I, because both my first and my second husband are artists, and Ruth, because she collected art. A few days before she left, she asked me if she could buy my manuscript of quotations on art. I wondered what on earth she wanted it for, but didn't ask, and we settled on a price.

Shortly after she got back to London I had an email from her. "Why don't we do this one together?" and before I knew it, all the 'I's' had become 'we's' and the number of quotations had doubled in size. My twin loves organising and she rapidly compartmentalized the quotes and arranged with someone to have the book laid-out and printed. One thing we have in common is that we both work rapidly and are rather sloppy with details. "Editor? Editor?" she scoffed, when I suggested it might be a good idea to run the material past someone. "We don't need an editor. It's only other people's words, just as they said them!" "But typos … " I protested. But it was too late. Before I knew it, a set of attractive copies of *Artworks* arrived for me at the village post office. I gave her full points for taste and design and merely yellow-tabbed, with a sigh, the pages where spelling mistakes and omitted words occurred. I might add that it was only after frantic, one might even say hysterical email protests by me on the night before the text went to the printer, that she had obtained some ISBNs for the series.

With the first quote book out, Ruth was off and running. She has a keen ability to extract material from her reading, as do I. Over the next couple of years we did eight quote books together. Even with subjects she knew nothing about, such as gardening, she still had a laser ability to select interesting quotes from her reading. The only way our method of collecting quotes differed was that Ruth would go out and buy 50 books on the subject we had chosen for the next book. She would then settle down in her Corbusier-designed chair, with the books piled on her Eileen Gray-designed side table, and devour them. I, on the other hand, would request the books from the island library and do my best to take whatever time I could from my other writing (that paid the mortgage), from the garden (I actually had one) and from housekeeping, in order to settle on my second-hand couch and collect my contribution of quotes. My pile of library books, I might add, rested on a great garage sale coffee table in faux oak.

Ruth and I gathered quotes on art, design, music, and gardens. We also found quotes on love, food, books and on life in general. I read hundreds of books and what seemed like thousands of magazine articles in order to complete my end of this twin assignment. For some of the books I wrote doggerel to introduce chapters, such as this one on Frank Lloyd Wright, which began the section on architecture in our quotation book, *Designworks:*

You know a building's built by Wright
Because it's never water-tight.
Tarpaulins a protection lend
For renovations without end.

Pretty bad, I must admit, yet Frank Lloyd Wright himself had said, "A doctor can bury his mistakes, but an architect can only advise his clients to plant vines." As I had seen one of his houses, in the town in which we lived in Japan, totally covered in blue tarpaulins while it was being restored, I thought I had enough evidence for the verse.

For some of the books Ruth allowed certain quotes of my own to infiltrate the more notable quoters and I hope later generations of readers will note my words of wisdom. It is more likely that they will wonder why the unknown author of a limp sentiment had been included. Nepotism has its time and place, I think.

Since Ruth footed the bill, she assumed she had the last word and I left it that way. The selection of quotations was her total contribution to the editing process. She did this ruthlessly (no pun intended) and manually! First she printed out all the quotes that we had collected. Then, with scissors, she cut each quote out and placed it in its relevant pile. As she did this, she would comment to herself "Rubbish!" as she threw the quote in the garbage pile, or say "Good enough," and allow its admission to the book. It was all rather like a judge sending the quote to the guillotine, or sparing its life. Ruth then proceeded to reenter the final selection of quotes back into the computer (along with typos). Need I say I had told her how to cut and paste, and I had begged my nieces to show her how to do this simple action. But stubborn is stubborn and she kept to her horse and buggy method for all eight books. I'm amazed she didn't choose to hand-set the type. Perhaps that option wasn't available.

In retrospect, a little less hand-selection and a little more spell-check would have improved things a lot. In one book she actually attributed someone else's haiku to me. I was furious, and wrote letters to *The Times,* to *The Globe and Mail* and to Haiku Canada disclaiming the attribution. Ruth thought I was being over-dramatic, exaggerating the error, and told me that no one would notice it. I demanded an errata slip. She was probably right, but I, rather belatedly, felt the need to make a statement about her carelessness.

Eventually Ruth bought an art gallery and lost interest in quotation collecting. When I suggested we do a last book together on science, she drew the line. Science reading is my hobby, whereas science and art held, for Ruth, the usual gulf it does for most people. I went on to finish *Scienceworks* on my own. Ruth paid for the publication and that was the end of it, until a year later when I received a cheque in the mail. My clever sister had sold the rights to the quotation books to the Courtauld Institute, in London, and there they can be seen on their own little rack in the gift store.

People often ask whether we differed in our selection of quotes. Ruth would say that mine were more homey, more Readers Digesty ... she actually meant "more North American," which seems to be a form of heavy criticism in the U.K. I retaliated with marking hers as rather pompous and ponderous, as if they were lining up for an inspection by Her Majesty, the Queen. I should report that our scrapping continues (we are now in our 77th year) and so does our mutual respect.

This quotation book period left me with the legacy of being unable to read a book without a pad of sticky notes and a pencil at the ready. In my most recent book, *Late-Bloomer: On writing later in life,* I included a generous quantity of quotations. It's not that I can't think of bright, or even witty, things to say myself. It's that I like to feel many folk are contributing to every project I do, and including their wit and wisdom is one way of doing this.

Quotations, for me, are those word-bites that in one small mouthful replenish my being, support my frail stand on matters and knock me off my soapbox when I am getting too serious about the world. I still keep files of quotations. Some are general and some are on specific subjects. These often stimulate the writing of essays and poems, for when I read a good quotation, I tend to have a dialogue with the quoter as their quotes raise further question within me.

What makes a good quote, a quote worthy of selection for me? If I am writing on a particularly topic, of course the first requirement is that the quote be on target. Secondly it must trigger a physical reaction in me – a laugh, a tear, a tremor, goose pimples on my arms, etc. This indicates that the quotation resonates with me – with my needs, my tastes and my philosophy of the moment. As in my poetry, I prefer the bittersweet, a catching of the heart-strings followed by a sharp dagger stab. For example, St. Augustine said "Give me chastity and continence" (how sad), and he followed this by the phrase "but not yet," (ah, there's the dagger stab). Did he really say that? This was probably one of Ruth's selections. The quote came from *Loveworks,* and while I continued turning its pages, I came across "Whenever I date a guy, I think, is this the man …" (my heart is opening, I can feel it). Rita Render, however, then completes the sentence with "I want my children to spend their weekends with?" and there's the required stab.

Oh dear. You'll be thinking I aided and abetted eight quotation books filled with cynicism and despair. But wait! There are also quotes such as this one by Somerset Maugham, "The great tragedy of life is not that men perish, but that they cease to love." and this beautiful Japanese proverb, "In a child's lunch box, a mother's thoughts." So don't give up on me yet, please.

Let's give the last word on the subject of quotations to Thomas Love Peacock who said "A book that furnishes no quotations is *me judice,* no book – it is a plaything" and I, with my notes in my left hand and my sharpened pencil in my right, totally endorse this opinion.

Compositions: Notes on the written word

Poetic Pause

Eating Poetry

Ink runs from the corners of my mouth.
There is no happiness like mine.
I have been eating poetry.
– Mark Strand

I have used this quotation once before, in *Late Bloomer: On Writing Later in Life,* but try as I can, I can't find another one that expresses the joy of poetry quite as well, so here it is again. I can just see the words hanging out of the edge of Mark's mouth – there's 'love' and there's 'moonlight' and look – there's 'disaster.'

Two things happened recently that reinforced the correctness of my choice some years ago, at the age of 65, to become a full-time poet. One was my annual hosting of a haiku retreat for a group of poets and soon-to-be poets. The second reinforcement came from the reading of two books about teaching poetry to students.

The first book, *Love That Dog,* a Newberry Award winner, is described as a novel. It is the kind of book that parents, grandparents and teachers love. It has heart, purpose and a happy ending, but I wondered how kids responded to this delicious tale of how a young boy comes to realize that poetry isn't just for girls. I asked around a bit and found kids also gave it a thumbs up. It is recommended for eight to twelve-year olds and the inside front jacket summarizes the plot in this way:

"This is the story of Jack
who finds his voice
with the help of
paper
pencil
teacher
and
dog"

I can't recommend it enough. The author, Sharon Creech, does not guarantee it will produce future poet laureates but that's not the aim of the story. The aim is to show how to make a connection between a child and that child's true voice, with poetry. In the book this connection not only validates the child, but is an enormous boost to his self-esteem.

The second book reaches out to a diametrically opposite group of students. It is Jill Solnicki's true story of teaching at a special school. Jill, herself, comes from a privileged background of a first-class education and a girlhood of culture, horse-back riding and other such activities of middle-class children. Her students come from problem homes and are often troubled and uneducated. On a Monday morning when Ms. Solnicki asks what they have done over the weekend, it is more likely to be encounters with the police, or a haze of drugs, sex and alcohol than horse-back riding.

Against all odds, Ms. Solnicki perseveres with her creative writing class and the student's poems at the end of the book are heartbreaking. This is a rough, tough book, but if those are the kind of students teachers are working with, *The Real me is Gonna be a Shock* is a book they can look to for inspiration.

In both books poetry is a way to open communication. In *Love that Dog* the poems the teacher explores (and Jack comments on) are presented one by one, as the class studies them, and the story progresses. In *The Real Me is Gonna Be a Shock,* blank verse is the key to opening the floodgates to the strong emotions of these sadly abused, neglected, and low self-esteem students.

Poetry is condensed life that can resonate with the readers' own lives to release emotions. For this reason alone, I beg any readers who are encouraging children to appreciate poetry, to read them lots of poetry that speaks to them of their joys and fears. Don't bother explaining the poem to them, but choose poems that make them laugh, tear up, be angry at injustices, or just become very quiet and thoughtful. Then, without telling them how difficult it is to write a good poem, ask them to write ... and write they will. The form, line breaks, word choice and other such matters can be left until later.

I have had a good bit of experience teaching haiku in schools and the sight of a manila envelope still scares me. Not because it contains a rejection of a manuscript by a publisher, but because it might contain 30 haiku, written in strict and inappropriate five, seven, five syllable form from an earnest class of students and an even more earnest teacher. Have I failed once more, I ask myself? Recently I was asked to teach ten young girls about haiku. They arrived at our house and gathered around the kitchen table. Short of sitting in a meadow, the kitchen table is a great place for teaching haiku. I explained how we were going to catch a moment, and a few of the girls cupped their hands together as if trying to catch a butterfly. "Yes, it is just like that," I said, and we proceeded to work out how we could eliminate the past and the future, thoughts and emotions and just stay with what we were sensing at that moment. Their results were varied, but just as they were leaving, one little girl turned around and recited to me:

moment caught
pocket unzipped
ouch!
— *Emily Carson-Apstein*

I gave her a quick hug for really 'sensing' the moment.

If I had to give only one bit of advice for the teaching of poetry, I would suggest telling the student to read the poem as if they were the poet writing it. I would then leave it for the student to wrestle with that approach.

When I am editing other people's poetry, I am often disappointed because it turns out, more often than not, that what the poet really is asking me to do is to praise the poem and tell them how to get it in the next issue of the New Yorker. Yet I am, from time to time, contacted by a poet whose voice I hear clearly and who is willing to scrub and polish each of her or his poems. For me it is bliss to watch them work.

Recently, two of these poets have persevered enough, have worked, and reworked, and worked their lines again so that they had enough poems finished to be able to publish a book. Frances Astor's *One-Song and other works* and Allegra Wong's *A Pure Bead* show the signs of mature poets. Their sensitivity and fresh ways of looking at things are quite exceptional, but more importantly, their tenacity took them through to completing a body of work. Almost anyone can write one passable poem, but to write 70, or 80, that takes a real poet.

When people hear me reading my poetry at poetry cafes and libraries they often come up afterwards and tell me, with some amazement, that they can understand it. They say that every word was comprehensible, that the subject of the poem resonated with them and they would like me to tell them of

more 'accessible' poets. I mention my two favourites, Wisława Szymborska and Billy Collins and often add local poets, such as Tim Lander, who gives away his wonderful expoundings, in leaflet form, on the streets of Nanaimo and Vancouver.

If poetry is not understandable, what is it? I realize that there are many kinds of poetry from academic, intellectual poetry with abstruse references and abstract metaphors, to the simplicity of Hallmark-card poetry. For me a poem must catch the heart first, then engross the senses and the intellect. It must also have a mysterious element, a corner of the poem that almost, but not completely, shuts me out. This offers me a challenge.

And the summer haiku meeting? How does that fit in with the encouragement of poets? Perhaps I should offer a word first about the origin of the summer haiku get-togethers on our island of Gabriola. As one ages, memories come forward and overlay the demands of the day. One memory, that leaped up from nearly 70 years in the past, was of myself, and my twin, in the kitchen of my grandmother's boarding house. My grandparents, immigrants to England from the pogroms of Europe, spoke only Yiddish. The boarding house was full of foreign people and foreign smells and too much table linen, and bed linen, and giant cruets and laughter; far too much for two little girls who were being Anglicized as fast as she could do it by their class-conscious, immigrants' daughter mother.

On the occasion that came to memory, a Jewish refugee, let's call him Max, was standing with us by the fire while my grandmother rolled out noodles on the large kitchen table. He handed us a gift. We were perplexed. Why was he doing this? He explained that it was his birthday and that he always gave gifts on his birthday. We burst out in giggles and Ruth, the bolder twin, said, "That's silly! We get gifts on our birthday, not give them!" Recalling that moment in later years, I decided Max had had a great idea, and so I started to invite haiku writers to our small home on Gabriola every year around the time of my birthday. It has been a wonderful gift for me and I hope it has been for the attendees too.

Here's how an average haiku weekend runs. On Saturday, a motley group of folk arrive. They often remind me of Issa's writing:

a moonlit night; we few assorted cranks
fogies and halfwits
call the Name with thanks

Not that the attendees are cranks, fogies, or halfwits, far from it. Actually they are more likely to be professors, artists, housewives, house painters, librarians etc. (not that we can't all be cranks from time to time). My point being that just as the few remaining worshippers of Amida Buddha gathered together in the poem, so it is also rather quixotic, at this time of climate and political upheaval in the world, to be concentrating together on how to catch moments. Or perhaps that is all one really can do, and maybe, by so doing, we restore the balance of this crazy world just a little.

When we have gathered, we sit and share what we are doing in the haiku/poetry writing area and then we go on what is called the ginko. The ginko is the essence of the haiku gathering. It is a walk through the woods to a beach close to our house in the hopes that the participants will be inspired by the natural setting and will be encouraged by fellow writers to write some sharply targeted haiku.

Whether they are sharply targeted or not doesn't really matter, because next we gather on our deck, with the haiku we have written drawn large, and anonymously, on sheets of paper. These are held up and we gentle, sensitive haijin tear them to shreds. This is by far the most interesting part of the weekend for me. As the haiku are dissected and suggestions are offered for their improvement, I begin to see that I know little of the craft and am amazed at how, each year, the art of writing a good haiku opens ever wider and deeper for me.

The rest of the weekend is spent in potluck (for haiku poets seem to work up a tremendous appetite after taking their haiku walks), sharing our favourite haiku and looking at *haiga* (haiku that have been illustrated, whether with drawing, painting, or more recently, with photography). We often have a small, relevant talk by some authority, perhaps on *wabi-sabi,* that element not far away from any haiku, or on *senryū,* that witty form of haiku concerned with human foibles rather than natural phenomenon; although both haiku and *senryū* finish up in the same place … the unsatisfactoriness of the human condition and the passing of all things.

During the weekend, participants open to each other by sharing their haiku. Haiku describe precise moments when the poet and the object of the haiku have become one. By losing ourselves in such moments, we motley crew of house cleaners, gardeners, teachers, artists and business folk, paradoxically enough manage to gain insights that send us homewards from our annual gathering with fresh energy and general empowerment.

There is a rather nice account of our Gabriola summer ginko in *Wabi Sabi for Writers,* by Richard R. Powell, from the viewpoint of newcomers to the annual haiku gathering. On the ferry back to Vancouver Island afterwards, Richard comments to his wife that he had a headache, was tired, but felt a light elation. I'm not sure what caused the headache, unless it was an overload of haiku, or perhaps too much potluck, but the light elation is what I always feel after a poetry gathering whether it be at a poetry cafe, a library reading, or just some friends coming together on a summer night.

poets together
their words echo across
the summer night

Whether I am facilitating poetry workshops, hosting haiku ginko, teaching, coaching, reading or writing, for me, poetry is the focus, poetry is the release and poetry is the joy. If you are a teacher reading this and feeling somewhat the same as I do about poetry, please read *Love that Dog* and *The Real Me is Gonna be a Shock*. I'm sure you could add many other books just as inspirational, but these two are a good beginning. See if they don't offer new approaches for sharing the love of reading, and writing poetry – both being very direct ways of restoring sanity to ourselves and to the universe.

A Further Look at Haiku

Having offered you a glimpse of our annual haiku ginko, let's add some more reflections on this type of poetry. As I said, each time I hear authorities speak on haiku during the critiquing part of the haiku weekend, I feel as though I have not spent 20 years considering haiku and writing haiku. I feel as though my haiku are a distant shadow of others' haiku and that I haven't the simplest grasp of what a haiku should be. And yet ... and yet, I know a good haiku when I read one. I know the shiver, the shudder, the sparkle in the air above the page. I know from all these that the haiku has hit its target, that intense moment that can explode in an instant to shoot you into the void, or certainly out of the rut you might find yourself in.

Why do I fret so over haiku? I have already explored them a little in *Late Bloomer* and spoken about them when exploring poetry above, yet here I am, still clinging to their form and beating my head against a wall until I can cut out my intellect and write a good one. I think that I love them so much because haiku are as **sparse** as a nun's room, as **condensed** with power as a nuclear device and as **bittersweet** as my favourite dark, dark chocolate. Sparseness in all aspects of life, a paring down; condensedness the ability to concentrate large ideas in small everyday things and the bittersweetness of life, that ability to accept plus and minus as the way reality is; all these must be elements that need reinforcing in my psyche, they don't have to represent (and probably don't) your needs.

And speaking of the condensedness of haiku, the shortest haiku I know of (and probably the most focused piece of poetry ever) is the following by Alan Pizzarelli from *Zenryu and Other works.*

buzzZ
  Slap
buzzZ

Was it Nietzsche who said "life is only irritation and death?" If so, then this is his haiku. Can more be said in three little words? It's true folks seem to put a lot of importance to the phrase, "I love you," but do these three little words really catch the essence of life as truly as Alan's? That is not a rhetorical question.

Are there requirements for writing a haiku? As I mentioned in my book, *Late Bloomer,* physical needs are few.

no paper!
I write a haiku
on a shell.

But actual needs are more demanding. Haiku demands you see with the clarity of a child. Well, maybe that is a romantic idea of children on my part, but what I am talking about is clear-seeing. Seeing without judgement, or intellectual comment; seeing without conditioning. Bashō expressed this when he demanded that reality should be shown without contamination by the ego of the poet. Well yes, what I need you to be is enlightened (whatever that might mean), for a haiku is a moment of seeing things as they really are. I know that that is a little demanding, but, oddly enough, I've rarely met a person who hasn't had at least one moment of extreme clarity in their lives, even though they were perplexed by it, and often so confused that they laughed, or cried, aloud in bewilderment. That's what a good haiku needs, nothing less.

Even though I've used similes to describe what I love about haiku, in the haiku themselves, let's have no metaphors or similes please. Western poets seem to feel that the metaphor, or simile, will help them define more sharply and refine the description of what they want to communicate. A haiku poet doesn't aim at hitting the target by those means. For haiku, the poet must still be on target, but must approach it obliquely, tangentially, by hints and through the mists. A metaphor may be implied in the resonance of the haiku, but you will have to search for it behind the very concrete nouns that declare what the poet has sensed.

Haiku derived from linked verses called renga, which, in turn, developed from a Japanese form of poetry, tanka. Tanka are full of metaphor (explicit, or implicit) and of simile. As Professor Sonja Arntzen, former professor of Japanese litera-ture at the University of Toronto, pointed out to me, in some tanka the whole poem is a metaphor. Over the years, these figures of speech became part of the Japanese literary culture so that when the word 'flower' appears, it can only mean cherry blossom and if 'grass pillow' is used, one can hazard a guess that a journey is being spoken of, and, of course, 'moon' in a tanka has to imply autumn. In this way haiku nouns, at least in Japanese, have 600 years of tanka metaphor behind them. The Japanese tradition, then, is of not using metaphor or simile in haiku, because each haiku noun already resonates with layers of meaning. This practice has passed over into the writing of haiku in English.

The point I make in my poem, "On Reading Diane Ackerman" where I deplore her overuse of metaphor, is another solid reason not to use metaphor and simile in haiku. If you are 'in the moment,' how can you possibly have time to compare it to anything else? Metaphor and simile imply overuse of intellect and that is something one definitely doesn't need in order to write a good haiku.

I came across an amusing poem by Ogden Nash that also condemns the use of metaphor and simile called, "Very Like a Whale." He probably didn't know about haiku at the time he wrote it and so doesn't mention them, but the poem is a gem. Here's mine:

On Reading Diane Ackerman

I read on, compelled
by her metaphors and similes,
until, finding five in one sentence
I call aloud "Enough!"
and lay the book down.
I lie and wonder why
she continually
says "this" is like "that"
and why she doesn't say
how "this" is like "this."
Bashō could show her how.
For writing of a "black crow"
on a "bare branch" at "sunset,"
he doesn't mention "black witches"
or "gnarled limbs of unfortunates"
or "dark curtains descending" once.
And yet his "crow," his "bare branch,"
his "sunset" are enough to tell me
all I need to know about
time passing, sadness, austerity
and the ways of the world
in autumn.

I can't quite remember when I wrote my first haiku, but I do remember distinctly, about a month after I arrived to live in Japan, demanding of my Japanese language teacher that we translate a book of haiku from Japanese to English. I suppose I had also been the kind of child who expected to pick up a guitar and play it without putting in the required 10,000 hours of practice, for translating poetry is hardly what follows on barely being able to stammer out *arigatō gozaimasu,* (thank you).

On returning to British Columbia after our two-year stay in Japan, I found that Japan had entered the B.C. Ministry of Education's social studies curriculum and, with it, an interest in haiku had grown. By this time I had read a few books on the subject and contacted a few haiku writers, so felt confident enough to write a book on haiku myself, *Haiku – one breath poetry.* It introduced younger readers to the world of haiku. Surprisingly enough it became, as I have mentioned, an American Library Association choice in the section for poetry for young adults and there I sat in a list which included Langston Hughes and Allen Ginsberg. To this day I have no idea how this happened.

By the way, is it clear yet about how you actually write haiku? It's really quite simple. Just tell me of one thing that, at this very moment, you are smelling, or touching, or tasting, or hearing, or seeing. Tell me What? When? and Where? Then step out of the picture yourself and let the moment write itself down. No more, no less. Or if you would like a bit more help, here's:

How to Write a Haiku

Details confuse me,
so when I see a rose,
although I do not know

its pedigree, I write down "rose."
And when I cut it,
I do not know whether
I should cut it on a slant
or straight, or under water twice,
so I write down "cut."
And when I put it in a vase,
I do not know whether it is raku
or glaze or, perhaps, good plastic,
so I write down "vase."
And when I see two red leaves
on the earth beside the rose bush,
I do not know from which tree
they have fallen,
so I write down "red leaves."
And as I set the vase
and the leaves on the table,
I write down

rose just cut
beside the vase
two red leaves

And although I do not know
the details of what I have just done,
the sadness of it all
cracks my heart open.

I'd like to finish this chapter with a quote from Wei T'ai that is applicable to haiku:

"Poetry presents the thing in order to convey the feeling. It should be precise about the thing and reticent about the feeling, for as soon as the mind responds and connects with the thing, the feeling shows in the words."

– From Poems of the Late T'ang translated by A. C. Graham

Poems at the Drop of a Hat

As I discussed in the chapters on quotes, I was recently co-producer of a series of quotation books. They were done transatlantic with the subsequent two ways of spelling and punctuation giving a jolt to the reader should they find the quotes on the pages less than compelling. To start chapters in some of the books, I was persuaded to do some doggerel, poetry with rhyme and rhythm. As I almost never write in any form other than blank verse or haiku, I found the limitation of ABAB entrancing and challenging. How to be witty, without being trite or superficial; how to be touching, without being maudlin, all in eight lines or less.

The word 'doggerel' comes from the Middle English 'dogge' meaning 'dog' and also, in some not very clear way, 'poor' and 'worthless.' The words one hears associated with doggerel are somewhat similar – clumsy, shallow, sentimental, of little literary value. Yes, that's it, doggerel cannot be taken seriously; cannot be discussed at length in literary magazines, nor be expounded on solemnly in programs such as the CBC's "Ideas." Why not? Well, possibly because of all the qualities listed above, but mainly, I think, because doggerel rhymes.

Rhyme, along with meter, was necessary in the days before the printing press, when verse was still in the bardic mode. They helped the poet declaiming his tale, and helped the listener retain the story being related. Rhymed verse was the dominant style until well into the 20th century.

How is it that rhyme has fallen so far out of fashion from the time of Longfellow, Tennyson and Wordsworth? Has its use in TV jingles helped its fall from grace? Or perhaps we are living in an age of headlines, where news has to be startling to grab our attention and rhyme is certainly not startling, it's predictable, as anyone can tell you who has ever listened to country music. Perhaps, also, we want to distance ourselves from Victorian morality as is embodied in Victorian poetry with its anticipated rhymes, monotonous metre and tons of sentimentality. Certainly two world wars, the Holocaust, Vietnam, Rwanda ... a seemingly endless list of tragedies, somehow makes that form of poetry seem not only quaint, but irrelevant. Formal verse has come to be identified with conservatism and free verse as more 'with it,' more vital to our times.

But still, rhyme I had to do when faced with the demands of introducing the chapters in those quotation books. In times of yore, and still today, rhyming dictionaries could be purchased, with rhyming dictionaries such as Clement Wood's *The Complete Rhyming Dictionary* often recommended. Nowadays, however, you can just jump on Google and there are sites such as Rhyme Zone and WriteExpress online, where you just enter the word and immediately be presented with a list of words that rhyme, or at least approximately rhyme. I was doing a clerihew on a friend the other day and entered his name, 'Welch' and got 'felch,' 'squelch,' 'Welsh,' 'belch' – a fair list, though none of them applicable or, therefore, useful.

Somehow I prefer to run through the alphabet each time I need a rhyme; in that way I never fail to link up with generations of school children, and that sets me in a deep and thoughtful place from which I have to pull myself back in order to produce a laugh, a guffaw or at least a small smile. Of course children's poetry usually rhymes and bounces as a small child does on her father's knee. Nursery rhymes, Mother Goose rhymes, nonsense rhymes are all acceptable until the age of majority is reached. Then rhyming verse suddenly becomes labelled as doggerel and demoted as outside real poets' endeavours. Padgett declared "the banality of badly rhymed English sticks out like a razor blade in Jell-o." Still, sometimes I wonder what unites a poem, what links ideas in a poem, and certainly what provides the final resolution, the final cadence, quite like a solid rhyme? Maybe all we have these days are maybes, and so no final conclusion is ever come to, and no final rhyme is needed to bring us back into the right key.

As an aside, I have a small confession to make at this point. I go to sleep while listening to country music. Yes, I know, this is almost as bad as admitting I write doggerel occasionally, but I feel it is not a great sin. The country song has the meter of a mother's heartbeat, and so, no matter how sad the song is, or how excruciating the rhymes may be, farm and guitar for example, I lie smiling gently, wafted to sleep on the maternal breast. Rhymes such as farm and guitar are called 'slant' rhymes and country music lyric writers certainly get away with a slew of slants.

People on the web seem to be rather shamefaced about their doggerel attempts and coyly list them along with other hobbies such as billiards, martial arts, meditation and taming wild horses. Yet folks such as Ogden Nash made doggerel so clever and witty that it almost became high verse. Certainly he took the pomposity out of things that needed to be said, and got home whatever message needed conveying speedily, although with some appalling rhymes such as: hypochondriacs/ Adirondriacs, nostrilly/ tonsilly/ irresponsilly, or other distortions such as: "Each spring they beautify our suburb, the ladies of the garden cluburb."

On the other side of the Atlantic, the doggerelist, John Betjeman, my mother's favourite, was everyone else's too, for his books have sold over two and a quarter million since 1958 and he became Poet Laureate in 1972. Possibly only in England could a doggerel writer achieve that position, although *The Times* comment at that appointment does modify the serious intent of the selection, "By appointment: Teddy Bear to the Nation." Another English doggerel writer is Pam Ayres, and while not reaching anywhere near the level of Ogden Nash, or even John Betjeman, she is certainly amusing, in a Music Hall kind of way; check out her poem "The Wonder Bra."

Forcing rhymes and words to match metre can be agonizing at times, but can also produce a wonderful release, and laughter, when it is accomplished. By the way, you might like to know that the word orange is thought to have no rhyme. Now that piece of information should have you reaching for paper and pencil determined to show your metal and come out of the closet to declare yourself a poet that knows how to rhyme!

Because a poem is witty it doesn't mean that it's bad, or that it's not real poetry. Laughter is just as much part of the human condition as tears. A similar situation to that of doggerel/ and serious poetry exists in the world of haiku, where haiku are taken seriously and discussed ad nauseam, whereas *senryū* are just brushed off. Yet *senryū* speak of truths just as deeply as haiku, just as doggerel can be as profound as Pound.

Here's a piece of doggerel of mine, on old age, that went into our quotation book, *Lifeworks:*

It's bridge and bingo, guided tours
round London, Paris, Rome and Lourdes.
Fleeing the winter, seeking the sun,
it's drinks in Nassau, Reno fun.
And when the hips begin to bother
it's replace one and then the other,
and trust your children have in mind
a nursing home where they are kind.

Weddings, funerals, anniversaries, births ... all are passages of life for which a poet is expected to turn a fine verse at the drop of a hat. Sometimes I want to drop the hat and run, and sometimes I don't. Often I will drop into doggerel form for these requested poems, but sometimes I stay with my usual blank verse. Somehow weddings and anniversaries seem to demand doggerel and a funeral wake asks for something of a more staid nature. Some cultures would vice versa this situation, and, on certain occasions, I might go along with that.

When a friend met a man for the first at a Nanaimo bus stop and subsequently married him, I thought the happening amusing enough to get scribbling. This poem appeared in *Segues,* and the bride and groom got it into their heads to give a copy of the book to all who attended the wedding. I was delighted at this sudden spike in sales.

Bus Stop
*Bus Stop (to D and R on their engagement
after meeting at a bus-stop)*

A bus.
a stop
a bus stop
a pause on a journey
and where better than a bus stop
to halt for a moment

take stock
await the unexpected,
along with the bus?
And where better than a bus stop
to meet a stranger
and exchange cards,
not knowing at that moment
her name was on the back
of his card and his on hers
written already
in invisible ink.
And where better than from
a bus stop
should cards lead to letters
and letters to an understanding ...
a certain understanding
filling that pause.
And where better than a bus stop
for understanding
to give way to love
as all pauses should yield to love
particularly those
at bus stops.

There is something compelling about poetry on demand, a challenge to meet a deadline, a challenge to write about the impossible, that I can't resist. I am not doing a daily poem, as Don Marquis did and who wore himself to death doing when he started the Archie and Mehitabel series, so a small dare once in a while can be taken up. Am I still that eight-year-old tomboy taking on any dare that I was given?

I notice that there are a number of poets on the web advertising their services for specific occasions. One actually indicates that you may sign his poem, although he only offers three revisions for $15.95, so you may very well be reluctant to assume authorship, for who finishes a poem in three revisions? Another poet says "you provide the subject matter, I write a poem about it." And then has the nerve to add "Piss easy," which it may very well be for him, but certainly isn't for me, particularly if I haven't at least met the person who is being celebrated in the poem. Once I actually wrote a poem in memory of a woman I had never known, but whose daughter I knew slightly. It was rather clever (in my estimation) in that I surmised what the mother must have been like by mentioning the appealing qualities of the daughter. My cleverness overcame my qualms, and I felt rather like many ministers must feel when they are offering an oration over a coffin of a complete stranger.

My twin Ruth has demanded poetry from me over the years; poems such as one on a marmalade cat that comes to meet its owner as their car drives up to the door, and a poem for a daughter's wedding. Both reasonable demands, and anyway I owe her.

To Amber

To her keepers' needs no attention she pays,
This marmalade cat who goes her own ways.
When the shutters are raised in the morning she will
Be seen waiting breakfast, alert on the sill.
Otherwise she's elusive, indifferent, remote,
Save for one habit of which I will quote.
She sits on the wall, close by the front door.
The sound of car tires is what she waits for.
That tells her owner's returned safe and sound,
Sole hint of affection that in her is found.

and for the marrying niece:

Epithalamion II

'Moon' and 'June' and 'Honeymoon'
for third-rate versesmiths are a boon,
but Aunt and Uncle oft aspiring
to more sagacious versifying,
offer the following humble rhyme
to celebrate your nuptial time.
As yokemate, helpmate, partner, friend
"marriage's a bargain – world without end."
So said your Bard and we agree
that it's a pleasant way to be.
So joined, united, hitched and spliced
the bond is really under priced.
Now that you're paired and matched and mated
let's spell out the fate you're fated.
It's pillow talk at early dawn
and wonder at a baby born.
It's wifehood, husbandhood together
with a touch of childhood for good measure.
It's sharing joys and chores and woes,
Sometimes the highs, sometimes the lows.
A knowing heart, a listening ear,
the joy of having someone near.
And words like 'tender,' 'gentle,' 'kind,'
are those that first spring into mind.
But lest you think we start to make
a total Eden, here's the snake.
Because there's days when minds don't meet
and stomachs may not feel replete,
and hair is messed and oats are sewn
and things seem better on one's own.
These days weigh lightly on the scale
(the 'ups' and 'downs' of hill and vale),
because the measure of success
in marriage we will now confess
is of a more holistic nature

when judging either mate you're
certain to take in the total
kit, caboodle, works and vote you'll
find you're sailing way ahead
when all's considered – board and bed
and smiles when you come in the door
and hearts that open more and more.
By now you'll know that we approve
your step, decision, choice and move.
So we'll sign off with kind regards
no letter, email, fax or cards
but greetings of the loving kind
and hopes you'll keep these lines in mind
appreciating the solid bedrock
provided by the state of wedlock.

Wince, wince, wince.

The marriage has since been terminated, but I would deny in court that the quality of my poem had anything to do with that.

Poetry Preferences

I've just read Dennis Lee's essay on Al Purdy, and while his analysis is a little academic for me, his admiration is right on. I love poets who generously acknowledge the skill of other poets. My publisher was rather surprised when I mentioned that I often go to poetry book launches. Is it possible that my admiration for, and desire to support anyone pulling off a good poem, is not shared by other poets? Actually, I love that moment, when reading others' poetry, that I am able to call out, "How I wish I had written that myself!"

New poets are advised to read poetry until it is coming out of their pores. This is when they are 'finding their voice.' The poets with whom these apprentice poets resonate, can then become role models. The right role model at the right time can mean the difference between the making of a poet, and that of a fine poet. I should mention, however, that role models do not, and should not, stay role models. That is not their function, they should beckon you, guide you and urge you on, but when you have found your own voice, the role model should fade into the wallpaper like some exorcised ghost. It has done its purpose.

I no longer read poetry with such hungry searching, but still would like to pay homage to a few poets who helped me along the way. It's hard to know what attracts you to a poet, yet we all have our favourites. Mark Strand states that "poetry permits us to live in ourselves as if we were just out of reach," and it is this quality I look for when I read others' poetry. The following poem outlines my preferences, in general, when it comes to reading poetry.

I do not like

I do not like suicidal poets
although I'm not against death.
I do not like poems where
you don't know who is doing
what to whom, and where and why.
I don't like poems that go on
for more than four pages.
I have a short attention span
(the deficiency is mine).
I do not like poets shaking
their fingers at me and
telling me how to live.
I prefer to make my own mistakes.
I did not have a Catholic childhood
so no nuns in habits or
the habits of nuns please,
or priests come to that, unless
the poems are devilishly wicked.
I like poems that look friendly
and perch on one page.

I suppose it is my immersion in haiku that makes me appreciate short lines in other forms of poetry. Lines that condense great ideas and cosmic thoughts into about eight words are very appealing. For me, less is more when it comes to line length. Of course I must know what is happening in the poem, and to whom it is happening, and where, but that can be done in short lines just as well as in long. An alternative reason for liking short poems and short lines is my poor attention span. I am blaming this on old age, but have moments when I feel that had the diagnosis been around when I was a child, I would have been labelled ADD so quickly do I flit from one moment's absorption to another. Among my favourite poets – Billy Collins, Wisława Szymborska, John West and Mildred Tremblay and ah yes! Winn Starr.

I can't remember when I first came across Billy Collins poetry, but *Picnic, Lightning* is on my shelf of books that I am collecting, and from which I will read every day when I am really old. I once came across a quote of his, "A good poem expresses emotion for which there is no name. The only name for the emotion is the poem." That quote and the realization that his last lines tend to leap the gap between the humour of the poem and a stunning idea that will send you spinning, as my own try to, won me over completely. His poems speak of small every day things, and I picture him always on the lawn, barefoot in the dewy grass, with his dressing gown on. Here is a homage I wrote to everyman's and everywoman's poet; the one-time American Poet Laureate, (the Americans are not noted for good taste, but here's the exception) Billy Collins.

Ode to Billy Collins

I have the kitchen floor to wash,
the flowers to deadhead,
and a list of promising magazines
to index according to how much
they pay per word,
yet here I lie reading Billy Collins
while the house and yard and
outside world call for my attention.
Yet all I can do is pore over
Billy Collins and, even should
the universe, itself, disappear,

I feel I can only continue doing
what I am doing ... repeating
to myself the delicious lines
and turning the pages ... slowly.

Now for the Polish poet Wisława Szymborska, winner of
the 1996 Nobel Prize in Literature. Who can touch her for
sheer quantity of poems that hit the target? A fellow poet sent
me her *Poems New and Selected* a couple of years ago and it
rests constantly at my bedside.

Szymborska is a creature of questions and lists ... naive
questions and endless lists. What I like best about her is that
she approaches the big topics of life (Why are we here? What
is evil? What is it to be a member of human society? What is
it to be an individual?) with understatement and with
emphasis on paradox, the yes and no that exist together in
every situation. "Whatever inspiration is," she is quoted as
saying, "it's born from a continuous 'I don't know'." Her take
on questions is: "But any knowledge that doesn't lead to new
questions quickly dies out: it fails to maintain the tempera-
ture required for sustaining life." You would think she was
talking about a definition of science, but it is poetry with
which she is preoccupied

Szymborska is capable of taking an ordinary image and,
by the end of the poem, weaving it into a theme of universal
significance. She starts with a poem about clouds being of
endless shapes and sizes, just like a small child might observe
while lying in a summer meadow looking up at the sky. A
trivial thing, but her poem will finish with wider thoughts,
such as those on solidity and permanence. She looks afar then
closes in, or looks sideward at a concern, but always with
questions that open to more questions. From her poem,
"Allegro ma non Troppo;"

"Life (I say) I've no idea
what I could compare you to."

During the presentation speech, given by Birgitta Trotzig, for Szymborska's Nobel Prize, Trotzig quotes from Szymborska's wonderful poem, "Discovery" which finishes with the line, "My faith is strong, blind, and without foundation." How many of us have the clarity to say that?

And her lists. Poetry is full of lists, I know, but Szymborska's are exceptional – things she prefers, things she believes, reasons for praising her sister for not writing and her fabulous poem, "A Contribution to Statistics" which lists the number of people (out of a hundred) who possess such characteristics as "not to be taken lightly," "worthy of compassion," etc. finishing up with "mortal" on which she comments, "a hundred out of a hundred. Thus far this figure still remains unchanged."

John West, an Australian poet, first contacted me to buy one of my books (yes poets do this from time to time). We entered into a correspondence and I have watched his poetry, and his life, go around the usual hairpin turns that life and poetry can take. A nurse by day and poet when he can, he deserves a much wider audience for his compassionate, wounded poetry. I recently reread three of his books: *All I ever Wanted was a Window, Modest Lives,* and *Stuttering Towards Love.* Feeling I wanted to share these heartbreaking poems with all my readers, I decided to pull some of John's brilliant phrases from their sources and use a pastiche of them to praise him to the skies; all the metaphors are his.

Ode to John West

He hasn't seized life by its lapels ...
more strained it through a pinhole.
He's drawn to people with scars like his own,
hit by life and headed to death's bus stop
with safety-pinned cardigans;
mornings sitting in greasy spoons
and afternoons on park benches
near the ice-cream stand.
Terrified and fearful, stuck in
the square hole of himself, yet still
with pen and paper, he listens
to all the hammering world
outside his window.
All he ever wants is a window.
His integrity looms over the space around,
and his compassion is more than a cloak,
closer than a second skin.
He wears it when he cleans scrotums
and smells the sorrows of
the "never-returning-home" ones
that he sprinkles his days with.
His life spreads a paddock blowing green,
as his moments of reprieve, of trying,
of wonderful skill-less stuttering
send him homewards towards love.

"And Canadian poets?" you may ask. Well out on the
west coast, where I live, we have a remarkable bunch – Patrick
Lane, Lorna Crozier, Winona Baker (a leading Canadian haijin), Leanne MacIntosh ... the list goes on endlessly. I wonder
sometimes whether there is anyone who isn't a poet in this
lotus-land part of Canada. A strong female voice that impact-
ed me some years ago was, Mildred Tremblay's, a poet living
nearby, in Nanaimo. It burst into my consciousness and settled in a little awkwardly – awkwardly for me that is, for her

poems were like irritants. Irritants that might one day induce me to produce a pearl.

My favourite of her books are *The Things about Dying* and *Old Woman Comes out of her Cave*. Oddly enough I don't share much of Mildred's conditioning. I didn't have a Catholic childhood, nor her quantity of children (she had six daughters, I had one child of each sex and even though I appeared to have started working through the alphabet when it came to names, A for Adam and B for Beverly, I must have felt C was going a little further than I wanted). She explored Transcendental Meditation in the 70s, I studied Buddhism, and she works with images from myth and folklore – totemistic images. I rarely refer in my poems to those abstractions. So what is it that attracted me to her and what is it about her poetry that helped shift me a little? I think it was that I could sense an integrity that I wanted for myself, but that my posturing and ambitions, at that time, wouldn't allow me. She had a paring away, a stripping down quality that tempted and scared me. Luckily for me, aging just tripped me into this state of clarity (from time to time, that is) without me having to do much else. Mildred's poetry was an early sign to me of what was underneath my rubble.

I don't know whether you have ever done the exercise of writing out your favourite poetry. The actual step of letting the words flow through your eyes to your brain and down through your arm to your hand holding the pen has a most curious effect. It is almost as if you had entered the poet's mind when he or she wrote the poem. It is a wonderful thing to do, and I have often done it with my favourite poets, or with incredible poems that I have come across that make me happy that they were written. Of course, no matter how many times you write it out, it can never become your poem. Still, I recommend trying it.

When poets are asked which poem they have written is their favourite one, they usually say, "The next one." As Dennis Lee said: "I revolve around the things I haven't written yet; they're my centre of gravity." I feel that way too about my own writing, but when it comes to the poems of other poets, my favourites list seems without end. I may not fully embrace the poets, but here are some of their poems that I think are worth reading:

P.K. Page's "Planet Earth"

Denise Levertov's "Writing in the Dark"

e.e.cummings' "maggie and milly and molly and may"

Padraic Colum's "The Old Woman of the Roads"

Elizabeth Bishop's "The Art of Losing"

Stevie Smith's "Not Waving but Drowning"

Kenneth Koch's "One Train May Hide Another"

Ogden Nash's "Very Like a Whale"

William Carlos Williams' "Danse Russe"

Sharon Old's "Go Back to May 1937"

Stop me! I could go on forever.

I would like to finish this section with a poem by a certain Winn Starr, which I feel is worth a full book of many other poets' works. I tried, and am still trying, to trace this poet, a member of the Chaparral poets of California. I wrote to them, having seen this poem in an old chapbook the association had put out in the 70s, but to no avail. I would love to have known him. If you do or did know him, please contact me and I will give him full credits in the next print run.

Dancing Days are Done

Is it enough, as we stroll our way through galleries
at my portly pace, that I can be witty about
Cubism, and know how you should say Van Gogh?
Or, if you're patient, I can introduce you to a genuine
city councilman or hold forth on second-hand Marx, or
tell you how I got my Rhineland campaign star,
while we rest and I stroke your back and you run
your fingers thru my chest-pelt (It's getting
gray, too, you know). and I remember the summer of '42
(No enticing widows, but I had an entertaining
appendectomy).

We can go to the park with my kids on visiting days –
(My kids – her kids – never can be our kids.)
But I know a Schubert Lieder, and Sundays (if you
choose)
you can watch me sing in my blue robe
(They never give me solos.) and when we're alone I can
sing you "Night and Day" or recite "The Rubaiyat" or
my latest or next to latest poem.

Or you can listen to us poets drink wine all night and
watch us manoeuvre to be next to read, or dine at home
on cheap stuff with funny spices when my kid's ortho-
dontist has to be paid and swap recipes without my
having to admit I never really tasted bouillabaisse.

We could go out someplace for coffee – I'm
good at going out for coffee.
Is it enough?
    – Winn Starr

I suppose most poets can write one poem of genius and I
suspect this was his.

Back
to the
Middle

The Mystery of Subtraction

My father always claimed an addition was better than a subtraction (I suppose he was talking about his bank account, or having babies, but I am in no way certain). Now that he is dead, I cannot reach him for clarification of that statement, and now that I am approaching the 'later' years myself, I can find all kinds of examples where an addition is far less desirable than a subtraction. Being an ornery sort of child, I bet I told him so then. He would probably have scolded me for disagreeing with him, because it is a constant childhood memory, probably applying to both my parents, and my two stepsisters, that my retort to their seemingly dogmatic statements was "You can't stop me thinking." Which was, of course, both my blessing and my curse in later life. A blessing in that I always had a quick draw for someone trying to beat me down with a written-in-stone argument. The curse? My position did rather accentuate the importance of my mind over my body as a tool to deal with life's contingencies, and a mind is not always what is needed.

I mention all this in order to blame my father for the fact that I can't write a detective story. For a detective story depends on a crime, and that crime is more often than not, murder … a definite subtraction. My father conditioned me against being able to write in that genre (and that's my story and I'm sticking to it).

Moreover I have never lived in what Nathaniel R. Fowler calls "an atmosphere of crime," so even if I did start a detective story, I would be sure to trip on the details and be uncertain of how the weapon of dispatchment should, or could, be used. In my life, I have known two people who were murdered; one from my high-school dance class (only, I should assure you, the young gentleman in question was in London when he died, rather than at the weekly well-chaperoned dance lesson that I attended). The other person had once stood in the middle of the road and called me a dirty Jew. This bewildered me, for I didn't really know clearly what a Jew was at that time, and I thought she was saying those words because I rarely cleaned my teeth. When she grew up, she became a sex-trade worker and the killing occurred within the context of her job. I didn't view it as sweet revenge because I knew, even as I had as an eight-year old, that she, as a similar eight-year old to myself, had been confused and didn't really mean to be mean to me personally (or so I hoped).

I read detective stories avidly, my favourite authors being P.D. James with her detective Dalgleish (after all, he is also a poet) and Elizabeth George with Lynley (as I was brought up in England, the class difference between him and Havers plucks a familiar string). My all-time favourite, though, is Anne Perry and I am collecting her books. These days when the most intimate of family scandals blaze across our news media, it's rather nice to have them revealed more slowly in the pages of Perry's books. The Victorian period, the time when her books are set, was for her "the end of history, and the beginning of the Modern World." I am usually so wrapped up in her two couples, Charlotte and Pitt in one set of stories and Monk and Hester in the other, that I don't really care who dunnit in the end. Of course I loved the way first contact developed into love in both cases. Really, if I didn't have doubts about true love's existence, I would be better off wasting my non-writing hours on reading true romances. For true romances, however, you have to believe, and I don't. It's just like unicorns.

Of course Sherlock Holmes, as one of the earliest detectives, has been a long time with me. I have read and reread Sherlock Holmes mysteries at three points in my life – my young adolescent years, my young motherhood years and now that I'm approaching old age, sickness and, the inevitable, death. Looking back, all that seems to link these three periods for me is the big sense of mystery and awe at my body changes. In my teens, my body was going berserk, in motherhood, it had swollen and deflated almost irrespective of me, and now, as I age, again my body is changing; this time rusting outside and within. All three periods were happy times – the freshness of my youth, the motherness of my nursing body and the dropping of muscles and pretences that comes with age. The three periods also filled me with horror as my body careened out of control into breasts and acne, into first distended stomach and then contracted stomach, and now, into minus one breast and liver spots. This beauty, this mystery and this horror all whirled around at each time and I guess I sublimated them into the mystery, horror and pleasure of the resolution of the detective story. The story gives a solution that I could not, and still cannot, find in my daily life as I struggle to sort out the clues as to why I am here and what it is all about.

The golden age of detective stories was actually dominated by women writers – Agatha Christie, Ngaio Marsh, Dorothy Sayers et al. Even today I can enjoy their standard plot – a group of people gathered together, usually in a drawing room; a murder occurs, maybe two. The police are called in. An eccentric, but brilliant, detective (often an aristocrat) arrives. The group is re-gathered in the same drawing room, and the detective points his finger. Ah those were the days!

P.D. James and Elizabeth George carry on the tradition of fine women detective story writers and Lynley still carries the aristocratic (or at least gentlemanly) banner of Lord Peter Wimsey and Roderick Alleyn, emblazoned with slightly more technical methods of detection, however.

Recently I read the strangest history of crime writing, Ernest Mandel's *Delightful Murder*. He certainly knows his facts, albeit they come out a little Trotskyish (which is not surprising seeing that he had been at one time a Trotskyite, and an icon of the student movements of the 60s) with much mention of 'capitalist bourgeois' sounding slightly displaced from some previous era as he talks about detective stories being the "opium of the new middle class." Mandel does, however, ponder on the phenomenon of the widely read detective story, "We can only shake our heads, sigh, and wonder how tens of millions of devotees can calmly and uncritically *enjoy* reading ten, twenty, thirty episodes of frightful slaughter each year, about five hundred or a thousand imaginary murders in a lifetime." This made me feel very guilty, for I had never totalled my reading up so bleakly. However, he does give me a slight out when he adds, "Reading about violence is an innocent form of witnessing and enjoying violence – albeit perhaps in a shuddering, shameful and guilt-ridden way." If only reading about violence totally sublimated its acting out ... but wars continue. Raymond Chandler, he of the very violent Roman noir, wisely points out that "the detective story has to be written in a certain spirit of detachment: otherwise nobody but a psychopath would want to write it, or read it."

One of my favourite mysteries is one of the first ones ever written, Wilkie Collin's *The Moonstone*. Since 1868, it has never been out of print. It was originally published in serial form and so the end of each section is a real cliff-hanger. How people must have eagerly awaited the next instalment. As in other stories written at that time, the colonies were presented as exotica. The raw frontiers of North America also appear as strange, rough settings, in Holmes' and other Victorian detective stories, which, of course, they were. In contrast, the nice thing about Alexander McCall Smith's Botswana series, with Precious Ramotswe, is that their setting is ordinary, everyday Botswana. North Americans are rarely able to read about ordinary folks going their ordinary ways in African society. The series provides moral certainty and heart-warming resolutions. I found them very appealing until, in later ones, formula took over. That's often the trouble with series. In McCall Smith's books, the crimes are white-collar, or crimes of social misbehaviour – hardly criminal. Not involving bodily subtractions, perhaps such a sub-genre of detective story would leave me little room for excuse for not writing.

One of the reasons that I read detective stories is because I am fascinated with the strategies and problem solving involved (although every writer of the genre, I feel, cheats by leaving out clues, or by bringing in alien solutions in the chapter before the last one – even dear Agatha). I also read the genre because I am not large enough to solve the injustices of the world on my own, so every little correction of bad, which the detective does by solving the crime, is one up for us all here in the Planet Earth survival rooting section.

Now, a little more about the cheating ... this might include a missing clue, a clue not shared, a beyond-belief coincidence, a totally uncalled for confession, or a relative that pops up from nowhere at the end (how could we possibly know they would?) Detective stories are a race between the reader and the writer as to who will solve the crime first. For this reason detective stories must play fair and have a level playing field; but they never do. The criminal can trick the detective, but the author should at least give the reader a fair chance of saying half way through, "It was the butler," and at the end being able to smugly confirm this with, "See, I told you I was right." We get so few chances to say those words.

I always complain about having to suspend belief at some part of the story, but I suppose that is the price to pay for a page-turning yarn. And that is another reason why I can't write detective stories, because although I am willing to make allowances for other authors' illogical moves, I am much harder on myself. For example, if I need to have three people appearing on the steps of the town hall at the same time in order to further a story, I will fret and fuss until I find a logical reason for them to meet in this way. And if I can't, yet one more of my stories enters the wastepaper basket.

Many detective stories just unfold and the detective seems to fall carelessly onto clues – not from any clever deductions he or she has made. Oddly enough when I spoke to a retired police officer, complaining about just this, he enlightened me by telling me that that is actually how most crimes are solved! This news of the lackadaisical way of behaving by the police force was reinforced by a report of similar behaviour on the part of an author, for I heard echoes of this carelessness in John Connolly's account of how he writes a detective story: "When I write the first draft, the experience is very similar to the one that the reader will eventually have when he, or she, reads the book." Connolly and his detective are both solving the mystery as the book gets written.

Today's detective book reflects, rather depressingly, law enforcement as a labour of Sisyphus ... endless bad cops, unscrupulous business men, wayward politicians. The detective is a hero in the tragedy, the tragedy being that as soon as one crime is solved, like endlessly sown Gorgon's teeth, others jump onto centre stage.

Putting all this reflection on society aside for the moment, (and it's not easy to do), I would like to move into purely intellectual gear and return to things I consider cheating, or at least poor writing, by writers of detective stories:

- The culprit shouldn't be brought into the story in the last chapter – no twin brother, or sister, suddenly appearing to allow the accused to be declared totally innocent.

- Chunks of philosophy have no place in a detective story. It always used to amuse me that Michael Creighton would alternate violent sex and torture scenes with a sedate essay on, say, Japanese foreign trade, or the influence of pharmaceutical firms on science faculties.

- There should be no fantasy method of murdering. No ghost strangling a non-ghost.

- Clues should not be obvious – no cigarette stubs matching preferred brand just left lying around at the scene of the crime.

- The resolution of the tale should be simple, as should the mystery, so that the solution shouldn't need explaining. The solution should leave more understanding, than misunderstanding. When we watch detective stories on DVD's, my husband replays scenes until he has sorted out who did what to whom. I have discovered that running DVD's backwards and forwards in this way gives me motion sickness.

- The resolution must be a climax, not an anti-climax ... the solution should not produce the comment "so what."

- Lastly, a personal preference, I prefer that stories not be about the extraordinary or the exotic. I like them to involve the ordinary incidents of everyday life that we recognize, except one of them which we don't, and that is the clue to it all.

And that's my last excuse for not being able to write a detective story, I have too many rules that put handcuffs on my creativity. Yes, I know, it is I who listed them!

On Not Writing a Detective Story

I've been 'not-writing' a detective story
for a long while now.
I don't lack possible titles –
"The Women's Institute Slaying,"
"Poison at the Salmon Barbecue,"
"The Gas Pump Killing" …
I even have a few first lines –
"She took the cookies out of the oven
as the Reading Club arrived,"
"The stranger stepped off the ferry,"
"The gulls all faced the same way that day."
They have an appeal of a sort, and
all, in good time, will be followed
by a second sentence, but inevitably
I will have to face the fact …
the fact that I don't know
how to kill anyone.
Not that I haven't been tempted
from time to time –
at age four when I reached out hesitantly
to push my twin down the stairs and,
later, when my life had become
a kitchen, I held a paring knife in rage,
yet still I cannot bring myself
to remove a character by unnatural means.
So it seems I am condemned to wait,
my pencil poised forever, along with
the villain's … what?

Writing, Travelling

You will find nothing here of preparation, what to take with you (the artist's waterproof pen, the lined yellow pad of paper, a Tilley's hat), where not to go, or dangers and illnesses for which to prepare. Here, I'm only considering why it's so much fun to read travel writing and why people enjoy, in fact insist on, writing while travelling, whether it be a professional piece, or a confessional diary. Even the dullest holiday maker at least insists on sending home a photo of his cruise ship with the usual "wish you were here" piece of intelligence for his friends and family to ponder on.

What spurs on this writing impulse? Is it because travelling sometimes jolts people out of their routines, so that they feel compelled to register (and share) their new experiences? Or is it that maybe these travellers are so well-insulated against change, staying always within their own comfort zone (a place in which most people prefer to travel), that they feel expansive and generous enough to share the quaint, weird and wonderful practices of the countries through which they are drifting?

As to the pleasures of reading travel writing, armchair travelling, with a fridge close by full of its familiar foods, is much easier than airport hassle, climate discomforts and the possible hazards of real life abroad. Or maybe you've "been everywhere man" as in the wonderful song Geoff Mack wrote, and that Hank Snow and Johnny Cash and numerous others sang, and so reminiscing is now your greatest pleasure.

the old traveller
leafing through *National Geographics*
in his armchair

But you don't need to go on a cruise liner, or up the tributaries of the Amazon, or into the deserts of Australia, to write about travelling. A trip downtown, or to the suburbs (if you live downtown) can stir enough thought to get pen moving on paper. If you stay aware and alert, the car/bus/train/walk downtown can be fraught with all the anxieties of a trip to an Everest base camp and have all the hedonistic pleasures of a beach in the Caribbean. Any shift in our environment, if we stay attentive, will bring a shift in consciousness; or at least that is what most of us hope when we plan to travel away from home base.

For example, one day I went by ferry from my little island to the closest town on Vancouver Island, Nanaimo. This is a mundane small town whose history is lost in the closed coal mines and whose future is not clear. We go to Nanaimo about once a month to buy supplies that aren't available on the island. The day just happened to be my birthday and the short day trip became a spiritual journey encompassing most of the rites of passage in our lives.

The Usual Birthday

Off island –
hardly a treat
but birthday gifts are needed
for myself – a kettle,
a new mop head, a flashlight

for frequent power failures,
and, from Eli,
a thoughtful stick of liquorice.
And meeting with friends –
wedding photos,
an imminent birth,
a new home,
a last big trip,
a solo sail,
a death – in the
middle of my birthday,
1:30pm to be exact,
news of a death
on our small island
has spread to the big one,
so everyone we meet
pauses, and speaks solemnly
– as if of their own.
And casually we go on,
on this my birthday,
to buy new shoes,
my first in five years,
and to treat the car also,
to a birthday oil change,
just slotting the news
casually with that
of the marriage and birth.
On this most usual of birthdays
all I meet, and buy from
or sell to, or hug, or
am hugged by take on
a Dante's journey import,
so that much later,
returned to our small island
and unpacked of this birthday's
dealings, it is not surprising
that we make love very gently
and that I rise to the occasion.

Maybe I'm advocating close-to-home travel writing because of aging limbs and the preference for my own bed and refrigerator at this time in my life, but that day-trip poem surely packed in a host of powerful small adventures that were worth recording.

A lot of the pleasure in travel writing is that travelling can give you a fresh perspective on life that you would like to share. You'll watch the skies more closely for colours of blue you haven't seen before, listen with fresh attention to sails slapping in the wind, or the distant sounds of a gamelan orchestra. Eating jellyfish in Japan, or durian in Indonesia will certainly spark your taste buds to attention and smelling the lavender fields of Provence will flood out any other scents you have ever smelled. By the way, have you ever dipped your hands into a bale of freshly sheared wool in New Zealand? It is the senses that make travel writing come alive. As Flannery O'Connor said: "The beginning of human knowledge is through the senses."

It's the sand between your toes, the ripe pineapple in your mouth, or the silk yardage (at Jim Thompson's silk shop in Bangkok) slipping through your fingers; it's the description of these that will keeps readers on the edge of their seats, barely able to stop themselves ringing their travel agent for bookings. Here is a section of 'writing for the senses' that I wrote at the same time I did the piece I have included at the end of this chapter. I jotted this scene down while staying in a Buddhist monastery in Rangoon, Myanmar:

One afternoon, a rather unspiritual idea occurs to me. It is the end of a meditation period and, as I open my eyes, I see a monk's rust-coloured robe hanging to dry against a yellow door. My heart almost stops. Have I ever seen such colour before? After that moment, things happen rapidly. Through the concrete grill work I glimpse a mustard-coloured gate set in a white wall, the whole being touched by the green leaves of a low hanging branch. Then I begin to see, I mean really begin to see, the colours of the monks robes – saffron, orange, plum, maroon, dark brown and the purest of reds. I am absolutely lost!

It suddenly occurs to me that at the end of the week I could go to Bangkok and buy silks in this range of colours from Jim Thompson's famous shop. Using them I would design *The Buddhist Collection,* which would devastate the fashion world. Later I have the temerity to confide my idea to the little nun, my chaperone, who, is herself dressed in apricot and dull orange, a marvellous combination. My plan doesn't faze the nun at all. She proceeds to show me how her shirts are cut, and I note the diamond shape inserts in the armpits and the fastening toggles. We share my golden, saffron, scarlet silken secret.

Later, I picked up on this sensual passage as a way to finish the travel piece on Myanmar, adding a touch of philosophy, as is my wont:

"But what of the silk?" you may remind me. "What of the reds and oranges and ochres splashed against the white?"

There was the arising of the silk.
There was the coming into being of the silk.
There was the passing away of the silk.

Travel writers have to make only one thing clear, and that is why one would want to visit, or at least want to read about, the place they are describing. If people about to buy tickets are reading the book, they will want to know the essence of a place quickly to see whether to go ahead and purchase the tickets, or not. The same applies for readers who are going nowhere, for they will want to know whether to turn the page and learn more of this fascinating place, or whether to shut the book. Travel books can focus on a special interest – Maori crafts at Rotorua, New Zealand; theatre at Stratford, Ontario or England; whale watching at Tofino, British Columbia; art at the Guggenheim at Bilbao. The writer could also be attracted, and attract the reader, with the historical associations of a place – gold at Barkerville, pioneering days in the Australian outback, the Egyptian dynasties, the Heian court in Kyoto. Travel writing with sports as a focus pulls skiers to Whistler, kayakers to the west coast, cyclists to France and mountain climbers to the Himalayas. Food-focussed travel writing attracts to the place whose palate is being described – Chinese, Thai or Japanese aesthetics, cowboy steaks, Italian pasta and of course wines in France (and Italy, Australia, British Columbia and California).

Take Ronald Wright's brilliant book on his travels in Peru, *Cut Stones and Crossroads,* in which he weaves Inca history, the Spanish conquest and his own travels into a rich *liclla,* a woven Andean shawl. His interest in folk music is another thread that winds through the book making his writing relevant and authentic. Lest this sound too serious, his wit and optimism keep us from sinking with the campesinos, who have become, as he says, "beggars in their own land." Mr. Wright, as a youngish, probably limited-income traveller, had his priorities straight (stomach first,) for instead of immediately filling us with awe at his viewing of the ruins of Macchu Picchu, he tells us that he neither ascended to the sun altar, nor descended to the Cave of the Moon but went straight to the restaurant and had a big breakfast, followed by eating the toast left behind by an elderly couple at the next table.

This kind of travel writing pulls you willingly along as the writers share their interests with intensity, trusting their enthusiasm will hook you. But there is also the travel writer who details the hazards of the journey; the hundred thousand prostrations on the way to Lhasa as it were. It is the onerous, rough path that captivates. And you nod your head in agreement, as you lie cosied in your lounger, turning the pages as the travel saga draws you into a tale of unknown terrors and extreme physical testing.

You don't need to love travel in order to be a travel writer. I know a 'crabby traveller' who writes grumpy, complaining and outrageous travelogues (she is not employed by a travel agency, that's for sure) that often hit a needed target. Her grumbling is usually softened by wit. Wit in travel writing should never be at the expense of the host country, however. One might recall all George Mikes' crude drawings of racial characteristics in his series *How to be an Alien,* which perhaps seemed amusing in the 50s, but now seems tragic. Better to keep the jokes on yourself and the pratfalls also. This kind of writing does, however, highlight a problem of travelling, for first encounters depend on past prejudices, and often one does not get past the first encounter before one chooses to flee. This is a natural reaction. Yet a good travel writer will go past the first, second and even third encounter in order to fill the stranger out, (after all you are a stranger too) to see him, or her, clearly in their own setting.

Speaking of strangers, I have heard Japanese tourists in Vancouver use the word *gaijin* – 'foreigner' when they were talking about Canadian citizens, who've possibly lived here for generations. I think this was when Japan did seem to be buying up the country, so I suppose it could have been taken as some kind of omen.

Some writers (and also vacationers) prefer to be well prepared before they go on a trip, and so they gather books and make notes. Reading about the place to be visited certainly cuts down on the time taken in trying to locate things you want to see, customs you need to acknowledge, and right times to be there for festivals. But, on the other hand, it may tell you too much and you may lose freshness by being influenced by what you are reading; seeing what you are going to see through another writer's eyes.

Still, a little preparation may save your skin. My husband and I, eager to see the wonders of Ancient Crete, didn't bother to read up on what was going on in present day Athens and so spent an uncomfortable night in a hotel there. There were mobs of people ranged around outside with loud speakers bellowing some undecipherable (as we don't speak Greek) exhortations and the army and police were very present. We never did find out what was going on. It was a case of innocents abroad travelling unscathed. Another time we planned to travel from Australia to some islands I am unwilling to name and found we had arrived late on a day when, for some reason, there was a curfew. People still on the streets, after our arrival hour, would apparently be stoned, if not shot. I always meant to go back to our New Zealand travel agent who booked that date and demand my money back, but somehow I never saw New Zealand again, as other travel plans crowded such a return out of the picture.

The other juggling act beside deciding whether or not to research, is to decide whether or not to take notes while you are experiencing an event. Taking notes is a sure way not to experience what is going on, but, if you don't take notes, how are you going to remember details? Too many notes and you'll have no colour, nothing of your own depths being moved at what you are experiencing. Too few notes and the incident floats off without anchors.

Did I forget to mention the first sentence of a travel book? It must, of course, ensnare the reader. Paul Theroux's first sentence in his book, *The Happy Isles of Oceania* is "There was no good word in English for this hopeless farewell." You immediately wonder what on earth kind of journey he is off on, and under what circumstances, so you have to read the second sentence "My wife and I separated on a winter day in London and we were both miserable, because it seemed as though our marriage was over." He finishes the book with his viewing of a total eclipse of the sun in Hawaii, saying "Before the sun emerged again from its shadow, making the earth seem immeasurably grander than it had ever been before, I kissed the woman next to me, glad to be with her. Being happy was like being home." Wouldn't that induce you to read the 527 pages of splashing around in Oceania with Theroux in between those sentences?

While the first sentence should be strong, going overboard with praise, or criticism, makes the reader suspicious. Is the writer protesting too much? "After all," you will say, "She is merely viewing a particular place at a particular time. A day later, or the day before, the scene might be entirely different." I remember reading Janis Frawley-Holler's book, *Island Wise,* in which she flits from island to island around the world: sand trickling between her toes, a Margarita waving in her right hand and not a cloud on the horizon. She could also be found wearing a lei around her neck, or sitting in a horse-drawn carriage which is clopping on the cobblestones to some quaint hotel or three-star restaurant. I remember feeling rather mean-spirited on the day I read this 'super-positive feeling' book and so I wrote to her asking whether she had come across any political uprisings of the underclass, gang rapes, clear-cuts, kids rummaging through garbage heaps, so on and so forth, during her travels to the islands. She replied and actually thanked me for liking her book. Authors can be very confused as to fan mail.

L. Peat O'Neil gives characteristics of a good travel writer. They include: "loves travelling, well-motivated, confident, friendly, curious, professional, researches well, has some knowledge of the natural sciences, history, geography, cultures, has writing and photographic ability, is healthy physically, as well as mentally and emotionally ..." well you get the idea and that lets most of us out, I'm afraid. Nevertheless, if you decide to write, go for it, even if your faculties are a bit blunted and your skills tarnished.

My favourite bit of travel writing is the first chapter of Jamaica Kincaid's book, *A Small Place*. It begins "If you go to Antigua as a tourist ..." and the rest is amazing and disturbing and, although I've been to Antigua as a tourist, I will never go there again without feeling totally different because of this piece of writing. In fact, because of this book, I will never go anywhere again as a tourist, or travel writer, without feeling perhaps a little uneasy, and certainly trying to be much more aware of the culture and history of the country which I am visiting.

Here's the piece that I took an extract from earlier, about a trip to Burma, before it became Myanmar. It is based on my past interest in Buddhism and a curiosity about the monastery where a Buddhist teacher had trained:

Retreat to Burma

One hundred and twenty dollars in cash, $1,800 in traveller's cheques, 1,040 baht ... I hastily write down every penny that I have left in the world. It is ten minutes before landing in Rangoon and we have been presented with custom forms to fill in, in duplicate. We land. My nose is streaming and I am running a high temperature, but nothing is running as high as my temper, for here I am at yet one more customs desk and this time a tough one ... Burma.

Everything I own in the world is in these two cloth bags; writing down what remains of my cash makes me feel even more stripped and vulnerable. I remind myself that I am on my way, with my husband, to meet my teacher's teacher. At his monastery we will sit in meditation for seven days, (the time we are allowed to stay in this country) and that is all that matters now.

But wait, apparently I'm wrong, for the girl at the desk is looking fixedly at me and is holding her earlobes. I am perplexed, but touching my earlobes in imitation, I feel my earrings. My earrings! I pound my humble little bags with my fists and then waving my wedding ring at her, I shout "Perhaps you want me to declare this too; maybe you think I'm going to sell it!" I am shaking with rage and even she can see that I'm more than a little distraught. She hastily brings additional forms and helps me fill in gold earrings, but it's too late. My first impression of Burma is rotten. She has her job to do, however, and stone-faced, asks me, "Do you have anything else to declare?" I turn my bags upside down on the counter. There are my patched trousers, my dingy panties, old shirts and one faded dress. "This," I yell at her, "this is all I possess in the world!"

The hotel doesn't help lift my mood, nor do the mice and cockroaches. However I remind myself that tomorrow is my husband's birthday and we are to see our teacher's teacher. This evening we are going to the Shwedagon, the pagoda that my husband has waited years to see. The reason that I am in Burma has nothing to do with the Shwedagon and very little to do with my teacher's teacher. I'm tagging along because I'm more than a little interested in finding out whether I'm to be a monastery widow for just seven days, or for three years, three months and three days, or for the rest of my life.

But first the Shwedagon. Showering and putting on fresh clothes doesn't help my fever much, but it certainly cools my temper. We get a cab and are soon at the Pagoda's base. There the scene is a cross between Lourdes and Niagara Falls. We struggle through soft drink vendors, picture postcard stands, masses of crudely carved Buddhas and all kinds of tourist junk. We take off our shoes and climb the steep stairs until we reach the golden bell itself. We stand in appropriate wonder at its immensity; 98 metres high and covered with nine tonnes of gold. All to house eight hairs of Gautama Buddha. But I am happy for my husband's sake that he is here, and that tomorrow is his birthday and we will be at the monastery.

Next morning I slip my little penknife under his mosquito netting and wish him a good birthday. He plans to give his very valuable knife to the Sayadaw, the head of the monastery, so I am replacing it with my own. I shed a few internal tears wondering whether this knife giving precedes a severance.

After breakfast, we wander down to the end of the road. An English-speaking gentleman stops us to ask if we need help. He not only calls a cab for us, but negotiates the fee and gives detailed instructions to the driver. I am delighted, for when arriving at the monastery, the cab driver doesn't just dump us, but leads us along the walkways until all three of us are bowing at the Sayadaw's feet.

Our teacher is well-loved by his teacher, the Sayadaw, and we, as his students, are very welcome. I immediately like the Sayadaw. He has a large-boned face with ears sticking out at right angles. His loud voice hugs you and his eyes smile from within. He calls for a visiting nun to join us. She speaks perfect English and soon we are chatting away filled with joy and contentment. Suddenly we realize that the taxi driver is still with us, enjoying it all. We laugh, pay him and send him off with many thanks.

We are in for a surprise. We have come via New Zealand to visit the Sayadaw, when, in five days time he, himself, will complete a similar circuit – America, Canada and New Zealand. We are shown all his travel plans including private letters from all the centres that he will visit; letters that certainly weren't meant to be shown to complete strangers, but there you are, that is the way with spiritual teachers.

The Sayadaw has not only been a teacher, he has also been a builder. When he first came to this monastery, none of the pagodas and shrines that are there today existed. The nun says it is almost impossible to count the number of buildings that he has erected: one time she counts to 70, the next time, to 73. The pagodas all contain Buddha statues; some standing and some sitting. They also house some amazing tableau of carved and plastered figures resembling a Buddhist Madame Tussauds. The Sayadaw had a vision and he literally made it concrete.

The nun is anxious for me to say morning prayers at the pagodas and it is during this tour that I discover my lady. She is the only figure that attracts me. She is Dewa Sara Swadi, guardian of the Dharma books and also of nuns. With her painted black curls, she looks like an Italian mannequin. I like best her gaudily painted costume and gold helmet. She has also been loaded with junk jewellery and a strange pink lace shawl. During the week, I actually go and talk to her a few times on my own and decide to give her a little necklace that, in my rage, I forgot to declare at customs and so will not have to account for on leaving. My lady's neck is rather large, so the nun places the necklace around the statue's wrist. I feel strangely serious about the gift and insist she place it so that the blue stone is very noticeable. The nun adjusts it to please me and, in a whisper, asks me whether it is very valuable. It is not.

Now is finally the day that the Sayadaw is leaving for Bangkok and America. There is great excitement in the monastery compound. To add to it, a monk is being ordained. Last night he received his robes and today we are all going over to the ordination hall to give him gifts – soap, washcloths, toothpaste ... his few needs. The place is swarming with the monk's children and grandchildren. On top of this, Sayadaw's benefactors arrive, bringing articles for him to take on his journey. He deals with it all joyously.

The ordination hall is run down and wretched. Our own temple is so spruce with all its colourful pagodas and liveliness and yet – somehow this temple seems closer to the essence; the essence of coming into being and passing away – and the suffering that comes from clinging to colourful pagodas.

Back at our temple the low tables are loaded with food. The women are shrieking and the children are running wild. Everyone is in great spirits. Suddenly the new monk appears at the balcony and throws handfuls of candies. The children jump into the air trying to catch them. The Sayadaw is anxious to get going. He doesn't have to leave for the airport until half past five, but the driver has already arrived at one o'clock. Who can meditate? The departure is not to be missed. The nun and I sit chatting. She has decided to go to the airport with the party and then will return to stay with us until we leave.

Finally it is five o'clock and the procession starts to line up. Bemots, little half-ton trucks with their backs converted into seating, are for the monks; a Mercedes is provided for the Sayadaw and his benefactors. The Sayadaw gets into the lead car and they are off. We press our hands together in farewell and promise to see him again in four days time in Bangkok.

On the last day before we leave the monastery, I am flipping through a book in a desultory manner, when suddenly my eyes catch the words "now if we could be spared the suffering of sickness, old age and death, wouldn't we all choose to work towards Nirvana?"

Suddenly everything becomes very clear to me. I wouldn't! I don't want to work towards Nirvana, whatever that state may be. I am growing old and will soon become sick and die, and that's enough for me to work towards at the moment. I am made of very ordinary stuff. When I hurt, I cry and when I'm happy, I sing. I can't live up to the expectations of the nun, the monks, my husband and particularly my old self. Even though the realization is no big deal, I feel an enormous relief. I'm sitting in this sweltering basement in a monastery in Rangoon, and, at this moment, there is nowhere else I want to be. There is also no one else who will understand me, so I tell myself again, "I am home, at home once more."

The Grande Finale

"One must wait for the evening to see how splendid the day has been." – Sophocles.

Others' lives fascinate us. We read about them daily in the newspaper, watch people being interviewed on TV, or pick among the millions of self-exposing blogs that now litter the web. We are even caught up in the lives of people who have never existed – soap opera characters, TV detectives, the Simpsons. Even today Sherlock Holmes gets more mail than the Queen of England; in fact people still write to Sherlock Holmes wishing to hire him. Actually, I would never think of writing to the Queen, although I have written several poems about her. Sherlock Holmes is another matter.

Why do we want to know so much about other's lives? Is it just what the Japanese phrase "sore kara" (and then?) conjures up; small children gathered around a storyteller wanting to learn about what happens next? Are you someone who reads the last page of a book first? Do we want to know the conclusion so that the puzzle is finished? Perhaps that is why we like biography – because the life being written about is usually completed and can be evaluated. But often the ending of a biography raises more questions than answers. Did he really father so and so? Did she really never leave her room for thirty years? Was their love truly so great? Who really wrote his plays? Still, the reading of well-told lives is a popular activity these days and perhaps it is as George Eliot said, "the best thing a narrative can do for us is extend our sympathies."

Accounts of other's lives can open us in compassion, and the courage with which people overcome failure and despair could inspire us to do likewise.

When we resonate with these other lives, we somehow get a widening of possibilities as we see our own life's events from different perspectives. Sometimes the accounts confirm our resolutions and sometimes they help us to see how our choices in life could have been, and still can be, better made.

Jill Ker Conway, in her brilliant book, *When Memory Speaks,* says that "autobiography is the most popular form of fiction for modern readers." When asked about this statement she explains that "in order to construct a lively narrative you have to select – just the way a novelist does – what events to highlight, what characters to develop, which ones to leave just in an outline." She continues to explain that the autobiographer is controlling what the reader takes from their history. Conway feels we don't read fiction the way our grandparents did; "we don't think of fiction as realistic any longer." She also points out that earlier generations "went to great novels to be instructed about life." She feels that readers don't do this any more. "So," she surmises "almost the only place you can go to start a reflection on your own life experience is to a well-written memoir."

Of course, unlike biography, which generally has a finishing point, even if it is inconclusive in some respects, autobiography, by definition, can never include a grande finale, unless the writer commits suicide and writes about it as he is dying. Socrates' death always fascinated me as he observed each portion of the body closing down. "Could I ever be that detached?" I would ask myself, and the answer would inevitably be "No." On this matter Sam Goldwyn, he of the golden foot-in-the-mouth, commented, "I don't think anyone should write their autobiography until they're dead."

Perhaps one reason why we like reading autobiography is because the priest in all of us likes to hear confessions. Our culture is becoming more and more a confessional one, preferably on TV, or, at least on the front page of our daily newspaper. We like to hear people's secrets and their regrets. Maybe we share them and admire the writer's courage in telling what we never would. And then there is gossip, which we are all forbidden as destructive behaviour, and yet we all continue to do, particularly on Saturday mornings in the village centre of our little island.

Some recommend an autobiography should not be written for revenge, but I like a bit of mudslinging this side of the law. It introduces a certain amount of energy into the writing. One thing readers do not want from autobiography is to hear someone wallowing in self-pity. I want to tell the writer, "Why should I be sorry that you have wasted your life? Just stop right now. There's still time to contribute something positive to the world!" Perhaps, as with all advice givers, I'm just talking to myself.

I don't know why most people I meet feel that their own lives are not worth recording in comparison with those that flash their 15 minutes on the stage. In my writing workshops, I hear constant apologies for the 'ordinariness' of the small memory that they are about to read to the group. Eventually I made it a rule that no one could apologize before they shared their reading (nor could they announce "This is funny"). As an aside, I actually don't teach writing in my groups. How can you teach writing? What I teach is self-respect … and I can't really teach that, I can only demonstrate it. Every life is worth recording, and I let my workshop attendees know that. Then I give them a reassuring pat on the back, or, when needed, a little kick in the butt, and off they go.

The other thing people seem to fret about a lot in writing groups is whether they would be telling the truth if they started putting their memories down. Since fiction seems to have so much truth in it, and non-fiction sometimes seems so full of imagination, this distinction has never bothered me. I'm with Picasso who felt an artist should lie in order to find another kind of truth. That does make lying almost seem deep and noble, doesn't it? Not that people who set out to write their autobiography consciously lie, but family members looking back on a particular event, will each remember a distinct, and often a very different version of it. It is called point of view and, in fact, all written history is really just points of view. Perhaps where writers need to worry a little more about truth is where lawyers might be involved. It's so easy to be witty about someone and finish up being sued.

Some start to write their memoirs to present their version of events; perhaps even to justify what has been judged by others to be a wrong act. Recently a writer gave me his autobiography to read. He had been powerful in the reign of a despicable dictator. Of course, it was a white-wash job, and I was embarrassed to read it and to think of the many people he had hurt during his career. Yet in the autobiography he presented himself as a kind of cross between Napoleon, Onassis and Mother Theresa. Luckily, most people are not intent on special pleading, but just want to write their life down in order to somehow give it shape, give it an order and ultimately, I suppose, a reason. I think we do this so that the future won't seem quite so haphazard. As Ken Burns said, "You can't possibly know where you're going if you don't know where you've been." Writing one's autobiography is also a kind of legacy, a way of living on. In later years people could read your memoirs, maybe get excited about your experiences, and wish they had met you. Yes, that would be a fine legacy.

A friend of mine has just finished a section of his autobiography. It runs to several hundred pages and concerns his years in the outback of Australia. By the time I had finished reading it, I felt hot and dusty, but most of all I felt acute anxiety about our car. A strange reaction you might think, but almost the whole of his autobiographical section seemed to be about his wife being pregnant and himself changing truck tires, pulling trucks out of the various mires they seemed to be drawn towards and deserting his ever growing family while he trekked through the sands in an effort to find spare parts. I offered the hesitant comment (one should never comment on a friend's writing) that the book seemed very Darwinian. When this was greeted with a blank stare, I plunged in deeper and said words to the effect that in the memoir he was striving to stay fit and survive and meanwhile he was also helping his wife continue the biological line (five times to be exact). I think it was not what he wanted to hear. The book is called *The Long Way Round,* which it was, and the author, John Nesling, pulled off something few seem to be able to do. He finished writing what he had set out to write. Writing an autobiography, or even a few memories, is both a daunting and a time-consuming task.

The other interesting thing about John's book was that he used one of the main occupations of his life, truck and car repairs, as a framework to hang the politics of the time and the struggle of immigrants in a harsh environment on. It made me recall how my love of music was reflected when I first started reviewing my life at age forty. Members of my family started to appear in my dreams, each accompanied by their own Wagnerian leitmotif. My mother's theme song was "Just a Song at Twilight", my father's "O Sole Mio," Ruth's "The Trout Quintet" or, more specifically, "Die Forelle" and my first husband's "Meine Liebe, Deine Liebe," Franz Lehar's wonderfully sentimental song. I could have written my whole autobiography using musical snatches to grab back my memories. That has probably set you to thinking of a framework on which to place your memories.

John put off writing his memoir for years, but he did have the wits to keep together his diaries and mementos from the period. When he eventually started to write a lot of the information he needed was there for him. Most of us procrastinate when it comes to summing up our lives on paper; it seems an insurmountable task. Lewis Thomas, the author of many brilliant science books, attempted to ease the difficulty of writing about his 70 years in this way: he deducted 25 years because he was sleeping, and then another chunk of lifetime because he spent it "doing not much of anything – reading the papers, staring at blank sheets of paper, walking from one room to the next, speaking a great deal of small talk and listening to still more, waiting around for the next thing to happen ..."

"Still", he continued "that leaves 11 years – 64,000 hours," which he commented "is not much to remember, but still too much to write down." Of course when he did start to write it down, it began with the sentence, "I was at one time, at my outset, a single cell."

I also felt the weight of the task and so, when the demands of others grew shrill, (for after all hadn't I written a pleasant little book on how to write your memoirs, *Memory Bag*, without writing my own) I tried a minor appeasement and wrote about my whole 75 years in 90 lines of poetry. I think I captured the highlights. For some reason when I chose to write my autobiography in poetic form, I wrote it in the third person. But then I've always felt a little outside myself, an observer of the strange and sometimes inappropriate behaviour of whomever happens to be in charge of that bag of bones that constitutes the person called Naomi Beth

Wakan. As Rayner Heppenstall said, "We are all largely fictitious, even to ourselves."

I recall P. D. Ouspensky's marvellous account of a day in the life of a European gentleman. It runs something like this: He wakes depressed from a dream; he breaks a mirror while brushing his hair; he is cross with a servant who has forgotten to bring a newspaper. He goes out. It is sunny, he starts to feel better. He goes to a cafe for the breakfast he has missed. He meets a blond there and life suddenly picks up. At work, he rings a wrong number and has an argument with the person at the other end of the phone ... he, once again, feels bad. He opens a letter full of praise and he feels mollified ... and so the day continues.

Ouspensky is asking how such a person can be a serious searcher after the truth, but I ask the question "Which of these many moods is the real person?" Or rather, as I quaintly put it sometimes, "Who is the 'I' who is going to die?"

Recently cookbook memoirs such as Ruth Reichl's *Tender at the Bone* and *Comfort me with Apples* have become popular. While I don't mention recipes, here's how I took a rather difficult few years of my life and transformed them somewhat, using my love of collecting recipes. I call it:

How to Write a Cookbook.

I've started to write a cookbook. Like people who try to give up smoking I can say that, in fact, I have started to write a cookbook several times.

The first cookbook I started to write, filled with quiche, custards, cheese and cream dishes, was the *Drumbeg House Cook Book,* named after our little house on Gabriola Island. I scrapped it when I was diagnosed with cancer and we switched to a macrobiotic diet overnight. That started the *Non-dairy, Vegetarian Cookbook.* I say we switched, because my loyal husband, Eli, didn't want me to isolate myself completely by my eating plan, and joined me to make an island of two. Our diet became so extreme that our friends soon stopped inviting us out, because they no longer knew what to serve us. There is an actual medical term for the kind of social isolation that extreme diets like this one produce, but, of course, I can't remember it at the moment. So, after deciding that having good friends was worth modifying the diet in the direction of the majority of other human beings, and being willing to take the risk that that adjustment might aggravate the cancer, we reintroduced fish and the occasional chicken dish into our diet. Once more we were in our little island's social whirl.

The cookbook title had now become *Get out of the Dairy Cookbook,* and I started to eagerly gather together my recipes that fit this billing. It was while doing this that I noticed something strange about my cooking habits. Even after years of cooking for a family, I still like to try new recipes, albeit they must be non-dairy – my present status. Someone had lent me a huge cookbook with probably 400 recipes in it. It sagged into my lap as my hands could no longer hold it up. I usually mark interesting new recipes with a yellow sticky note and rustling through the yellow tabbed pages, I found I had marked recipes with limited ingredients. "Yes" I thought "I am slowing down. The thought of assembling more than six ingredients on the counter seems just too much for me these days." The large cookbook, itself, also seemed far too much.

Suddenly the cookbook I was writing gained a new title and, at the moment, it is called *Seniors Get out of the Dairy Small Cookbook.* I am reassembling the recipes at this minute, so if you would like to cut out cheese, butter, cream and all that other weight-putting-on stuff, and if you don't eat red meat, and find reading the list of more than six ingredients per recipe makes your eyelids slowly droop downwards, and if you don't mind exempting the deadly nightshade family of vegetables for the sake of your osteoarthritis, and only want a few new great recipes, then you might just want to put your order in right now for my excellent cookbook, before it changes its title yet once more.

Note: Jill Ker Conway's favourite autobiographies are Janet Frame's three volume memoir, Gabrielle Roy's *Enchantment and Sorrow,* and James Merrill's A *Different Person.* She also recommends Harold Nicholson's book of essays, *Some People,* "for studies on how to develop character with brevity and clarity." I recommend the trivial, but charming, *84 Charing Cross Road* by Helen Hanff because it shows a picture of an obsessive book collector in a wise and witty way; Jung's *Memories, Dreams, Reflections,* because it recaptures my years of exploration of the mind and Ronald W. Clark's *The Life of Bertrand Russell,* because I like to read the lives of philosophers, mathematicians and scientists, but in a kind of immature, gossipy way. There is also Ann Thwaite's *A.A. Milne,* because his writings coloured my childhood so strongly and *The Diving Bell and the Butterfly* by Jean-Dominique Bauby, who became paralyzed from a stroke at the age of 43, and wrote this amazing book by blinking his left eye, the only way he could communicate. A lesson for those of us who whine that writing our memoirs is just too much work.

End at the End

The Problem with Poets

I have just read an article accusing haiku poets of messy lives. The author uses the words money, power, lust for fame, lust for control and speaks of haiku cliques and a false elite. As a long time haiku writer, I must say that I am shocked. I have never observed any of this in the haiku circles I move in and believe me there is nothing elitist about the odd bunch of mortals we are. As to money! Financially, haiku writing is a losing game, although Winona Baker did once win $1,000 for three small, very good lines. Surely the author of the article is talking about novelists?

It is true that poets have generally been seen as a rather hopeless lot, being able to get only insignificant or temporary jobs, if they work at all. They have also been accused of trying to alter reality by toying with drugs, alcohol and other peoples' partners. Then after years of seemingly futile writing, they often choose to end it all by throwing their bodies off cliffs and into rivers, or under trains with, oddly enough, a success that their poetry never had. As Christina Patterson, the opinionated commentator for *The Independent,* so neatly puts it, "Poetry has always attracted more than its fair share of the seriously unhinged."

Yes, I have occasionally noticed gaps between the beauty of the poem and the often tawdry life of the creator, but then there are gaps in all creative efforts; gaps between the vision in the mind and the result on the canvas or page, and gaps, as

Billy Collins tells it, "between how seriously poets take themselves and how generally they are ignored by everyone else." These gaps ... do they occur because we poets are more sensitive than other folk, and that everything is a little more difficult for us? I think not. Let's burst that bubble immediately:

Poets on the Whole

I don't recommend
befriending a poet.
They are, on the whole,
unpleasant people.
They live life to excess
and can break you open
with a few well-chosen words
(not to mention what is in
the space between the lines).
Worse still, they can stab you
with an invisible stiletto
should you dare to
interrupt them while
they are reading in public.

I once had a poet come to stay at our home whose poetry was fresh and fascinating. Forgetting the gap between the creative effort and the weak vessel that channels the poetry, I thought the poet would be likewise fresh and fascinating. The naivety, I must confess, was on my part. I felt the visit merited a poem.

How much can you forgive a poet?

A gift may shine like a beacon and the rest of the mind be
quite juvenile, squalid, ordinary, a wen of tackiness and
self-regard
– Diane Ackerman

How much can you forgive a poet
whose words punch you in the guts,
or break your heart in small pieces?
Can you forgive them:
trashing your guest bedroom?
staining your best towels with hair dye?
making and breaking endless dates?
long unpaid for calls to distant places?
the dumping of their emotions
in all the peaceful nooks and crannies
of your once tranquil home?
How much can you forgive a poet
for their odd well-chosen phrase
that melts your edges and
opens up the secret places of your cells?

It seems to me that poets, because they live in a separate
reality, tend towards narcissism. The onus is often on the
reader to put out the effort to enter the poet's world, rather
than vice versa. In generous moments I feel that possibly
their spinning around in their very own globes are necessary
in order for the poets to bring back such gems as they often
do. Withdrawal to a distant planet brings the possibilities of
new insights for ours. Anyway here's a little reprimand for the
poetry moments when self-absorption looks a lot like hubris.

Reprimand

So what you're a poet
And used to sit on the Lord's
right hand at banquets!
Don't tell me!
Or was it the left? Left more likely
since there's something sinister
about the lot of you.

Let me remind you "poet"
is only one of many four-letter words.
Most of you spend your days
pirouetting around your own navels.
The rest float at the edge
of the outer universe like hungry ghosts.
Just once in a while couldn't
you turn out a solid verse on
butter-churning or, better
still, on chopping wood, and
stop producing endless
chapbooks in foreign languages.

When poets aren't writing they are generally a big nuisance. Perhaps they can only be poets when they are writing poetry. Their loose energy, when not applying pen to paper, seems to hit out awkwardly like a poorly-coordinated child. And, yes, 'child' is a pretty appropriate word for poets at these times. John Kendrick Bangs gives a very amusing picture of poets in a chapter of his book, *A House Boat on the Styx*, when the club committee of the houseboat meet to demand rules to restrict the troublesome behaviour of such poet members as Omar Khayyam, who insisted on lying on five of the library chairs while writing his verse, and Robert Burns who occupied the billiard table and used billiard chalk to write a poem on the billiard table felt.

Of course post-partum blues are understandable, the blues of having given birth to an opus and feeling that possibly you will be incapable of ever producing another poem of such greatness. I have tried to describe this state in the next poem, but poets need to be careful that blueish behaviour shouldn't include dumping of frustration on nearest and dearest.

S=klogW

And having written a poem
my cells, just now swelling
with hubris, gradually shrink
and I pull in as if losing
the proverbial two inches
(that I will eventually lose anyway)
all in one instant.
My hair dulls, teeth loosen,
and muscles cramp as the afterbirth
period comes, and I lie
like some used-up odalisque
on our second-hand couch
wondering if entropy is reversible.

The biggest gap in poetry is, of course, between the idea in the poet's mind and the ability of the reader to 'get it' when it appears on the written page. If the leap from mind to page is too large, if there have been too many circuitous synapses and convoluted neuronic behaviours, then the reader will just not know where the poet has come from, and, quite frankly, not care. As you may realize by now, I am not sympathetic to academic poetry, where the gap between concept and print seems like that of tectonic plates fleeing from each other at a great speed. Elitist poets destroy poetry's accessibility and make ordinary folk feel they live in a different universe, or at least on a different plane. This is not good. The reader should feel empowered by the poem, not excluded. Academic poets drink, commit adultery, pray to their various gods, fail, succeed and bleed just like the rest of us. Why do they feel they need to wrap their usually quite simple, and often trite, ideas in a heavy cocoon of weighty, pretentious words?

For this reason, I am reluctant to purchase a slender book of poems by an unknown poet, for if I can't understand them, I will not only have wasted money, I will also have wasted time. Published poets usually don't have to buy other poets' works, however, because the practice is to exchange volumes. Of course ambivalent feelings can arise at such times, for not all slender volumes are equal. I am not an academic poet and my poems are not full of beautiful distracting metaphors. I am a bread and butter poet, a person in the street's poet.

I like to say who is doing exactly what, and to whom, and in what environment and I like to read the same in other's poetry. As Groucho Marx states: "My favourite poem is the one that starts 'Thirty days hath September' because it actually tells you something." I too like to be given some information in the poetry I read; information that I don't have to struggle too much to extract. So when I receive in exchange for my plebeian verse, a slender volume remote in tone and content, I must admit I sulk a little.

Plato would like to have excluded all poets, academic, or otherwise, from his Ideal State. He complains of the poet not being able to get to the eternal forms as a philosopher could. Nature imitates eternal forms and poets imitate nature runs his argument, so they must be far from the truth. Also poets raise passions and that rules out logical, clear thinking (such as that of philosophers.) Plato then adds the complaint that even though philosophers know the truth and poets don't, poets still seem to be getting most of the applause from the gullible plebeian public, and philosophers go unheard. I think I hear petulance firing Plato's exclusion of poets from his Ideal State. You can read all about Plato's views on poets in Jerome Adler's *Art and Prudence*, but I feel Plato is just underestimating the value of our sensitivity. Don't poets hurt more than other people?

Still that gap between Plato's abstract ideal, or the poet's first intimation of a poem, and what eventually lands upon the page is frustrating. Here's how I try to seize my daemon, (my tutelary spirit, not that biblical bad person) or rather, not seize him:

Seizing the Daemon

Seizing the daemon, it shifts.
The idea, once spread as the universe,
becomes a sesame seed in my hand,
and as my fingers close over it,
even this fragment of a poem
disappears into the void.
I must approach it sideward,
run my fingers towards it
as over a baby's stomach;
a baby I want to amuse,
but not frighten.
I can't turn away
pretending I don't care,
my daemon knows flesh from bone
and is not fooled.
It is only when I empty myself
of any wanting, of any desiring,
of any demanding for a good verse,
that my daemon will move forward
cautiously, move forward and creep
slowly towards my pen.

In my own defence against Plato's attacks, I can only present myself as poet. I think I am not a parasite on the state, as he suggests, and no more a liar (another assault on the helpless poet by Plato) than anyone else who finds the truth distasteful. I am a poet who tells of the street, the park, of little old ladies in cardigans and folks doddering around their gardens. In my poetry, I defend the underdog when he's down, and kick him when he rises on his hind-legs. I am really a very ordinary, everyday poet. Do I need to justify my existence more?

Saying Please and Thank You

Getting permission to include the words of others in your book is often a tricky and surprising business. For example, I had assumed because Emily Dickinson wrote over 70 years ago, that all her poetry was in the public domain and free to be used. I forgot that she only published a couple of her poems in her lifetime and that the bulk of her work was, and still is, owned by Harvard University Press. As the book for which the poem was needed was almost ready for layout, I quickly removed my very favourite Emily Dickinson poem, "How to make a Prairie," and merely referred to its essence. Assuming anything over 70 years old is in the public domain, at least in the United States, is a poor assumption to make unless one can afford a good copyright lawyer – and who can afford such a being?

To find out whether the material you wish to use is in the public domain, for Canadians, just enter the book data of the book you are quoting from into the Public Domain Wizard (created by Edusource, I found it through Google). For Americans, entering 'US Copyright Domain Office' in Google will get you advice. The author's life plus 70 years seems to be a rough guideline for finding works in the public domain, but there are many twists and turns possible. What's for sure is that a dead author and an out-of-print book does not give you a free hand.

Of course if the quote is modest, 'fair use' is a possible way of looking at your borrowings. But fair use is another iffy topic. If the quote is small, and is for non-commercial use it could be considered fair use. Quoting a few phrases from a book you are reviewing is definitely fair use, but a line from a Beatles' song or anything under the imprint of Disney may not be considered so 'fair' when you are bold enough to use it. At least that might be how Michael Jackson, Sony or Walt Disney Inc. would view it. Fair use is apparently only a legal defence, not a legal right.

I heard of a blogger who used clips from a Disney-affiliate program in order to critique the program's 'hate speech.' This critique was read by some of the program's sponsors and a few of them withdrew their accounts. The company objected to the clips being used even though the blogger claims they were used within the Copyright Act. This small use of copyrighted material by an individual had a negative commercial impact and so the use was contested.

But how 'small' is small? We seem to be swamped with kindergartens and individual artists being challenged over the use of Mickey Mouse images. Professor Eric Fadden took the bull by the horns and made an amazing small video, using hundreds of Disney clips, to explain copyright law and fair use. It is so wonderful that you should all stop reading this this minute and take a look at *A Fair(y) Use Tale*. By the way, parody and critical comment are two areas where original material has to be used, but "How much?" is still the question.

With so much digital sharing now the terms copyright and fair use are getting harder and harder to define. Large corporations are constantly trying to extend the length of copyright on their intellectual property, with Disney trying to ensure that Mickey Mouse never enters the public domain in any form. Companies are using various types of digital rights management now to trying to lock up digital media so that even fair use becomes iffy. But this is a can of worms that, for the moment, I don't want to explore. For teachers there is a hip video on copyright *Taking the Mystery out of Copyright,* and for you who wonder about free speech and digital control please read Lawrence Lessig's impassioned plea and check out the Electronic Frontier site www.eff.org/IP/DRM. Also see what Sony and Disney and Microsoft and the rest have to say about all this; it's good to get as many facts as you can from both sides before you enter the fray.

Now, getting permission. Once you have wrangled with the thorny question of fair use, you then have to locate the person who owns the rights to the words you want to use. This may not be the writer themselves. You then have to decide what rights you need. Do you want to include the brief verse in a one-time charity appeal letter, or in a full advertising campaign? Even if you have the copyright agreement in writing, if the agreement limits you to uses that do not meet your needs, the whole exercise is futile.

Whatever the rights, when it comes to getting permission, I have to tell you that there is waiting involved and also possible payment. The waiting, as with the Emily Dickinson poem when I was so close to publishing time, can be impossible, and the payments demanded likewise hopeless. In my experience the rule of thumb, is first, don't wait until the last minute and second, the smaller the firm owning the rights, the larger the fee that will be demanded.

Once, when writing a book on haiku, I queried a publisher for the use of three small lines (that really being the maximum a good haiku should have). He demanded $80. This was way beyond the dollar a word that the haiku writer probably got for the poem which I apparently needed to use quite badly. But not badly enough to pay that fee! For the same book, various universities and, if I remember rightly, Japan Airlines just waived any need for me to pay them. Usually a decent publisher will ask to be sent copies of the book in which his author's words are used and waive the fee. That seems reasonable.

I have one last reason to give yourself ample time to get permission. It is often much more expensive to get permission after your book or magazine is out than before. After all, then you have to deal with an indignant author's ego, and that costs!

My husband and I have a slide bank so we have been on the both sides of the permission issue. One company bought a one-time use of some slides, and then subsequently used them in a second print run without telling us. One night I woke from sleep with their name on my lips and, trusting my dreams, I made a quick phone call. This brought in the couple of thousand dollars that they owed us and a vague apology. This company also used one of our photos twice. The second time was in a new book which we hadn't known about, and so couldn't have granted them permission. Again a small reminder brought the necessary fee. This is just to present a case for the owner of the intellectual property you wish to use. Once someone wants to borrow your material you may feel a little differently about copyright ... I don't know how, but I'm betting you will.

If, after doing your very best, the contact person can still not be located and you are desperate to use the material, it's worth a chance to just go ahead and use it. A copyright lawyer may suddenly appear on the horizon, but that's a risk you are, by now, probably willing to take. Don't forget that the inclusion of another author's material in your book may very well renew interest in the author (whose work has probably been gracing the remainder table at Chapters) and so you have an excellent defence that you used it in the interest of improving their fame and fortune.

Once I wrote a teacher's guide for a book and, in my moment of hubris, thinking I had done a wonderful job, I sent a copy of the guide to the book's publisher. In return I got an indignant letter threatening me with a lawyer. I had, it seemed, forgotten to check who had the rights to producing any subsidiary material to the original book. Teachers' guides definitely count as subsidiary material, so I was duly squashed. About six months later, I got a rather fawning letter from the same publisher encouraging me to sell the teacher's guide. The publisher had suddenly realized that teacher's guides necessitate the teacher owning the original book and that is directly linked to sales.

If you just can't locate the copyright's owner but have shown good faith in searching for the same, as I did with Wynn Starr's poem, then it's up to you whether you wish to take a chance in the use of the required quotation, or not. However, if you get no reply from whom you assume owns the copyright, it might be safest to suspect that the answer is "No."

Ruth, about whom you have already heard quite a bit, just wrote her second book on an aspect of English art history. She is a wealthy woman, and impatient, so decided to self-print (including 40 colour plates!). She has a certain amount of the audacity that comes with money, and so didn't bother to get more than a cursory edit and certainly didn't bother herself with getting permission to use any of the quoted material in the book, or, of course, the colour plates. Oddly, for a self-published book, the first run sold out fast and she did a second. It was during this period that a firm of art-book publishers approached her to buy the rights. The purchase was on condition that all rights to the included material had been obtained. My twin boldly pointed out that she was an author, not an obtainer of rights, and so the sale fell through.

Should all the above sound threatening, or, more likely, unclear, I suggest you refer obliquely to the quote you need (as I did with Emily Dickinson's poem on the prairie) and don't use it directly. To assuage you, I should mention that if your use is small, such as using a couple of lines of a verse in a program for a church event, or if you, yourself, have a low profile, you can probably get away with it. Remember, the smaller the quote and the bigger your book, the smaller your chances of being sued, for the quote will be lost in the sheer mass of your words.

I should also mention that all the above advice cannot be considered half-way competent, and should be taken at your own risk. It would in no way stand up against a clever $300 an hour copyright lawyer.

Copyright infringement is when material is copied and attributed, but permission has neither been sought, nor, of course, obtained. This is not the same as plagiarism, which is something of which you would never be guilty, I hope. Plagiarism is to use others' creative material without putting any authors name to it, thus having the reader assume it is yours. The worst case, of course, is where you actually put your name and copyright mark right up against the borrowed material. As Clay, a much quoted, but unknown to me at least, web person, concluded, "Creativity is great, but plagiarism is faster." Plagiarism may be faster, but legally, and morally, it is a definite no-no.

In the years when I was a young mother, *Atlantic Monthly* was my preferred reading. I can remember distinctly the day I read a poem that I recognized in its pages ... but it had been attributed to a poet other than the one I knew had written it. It was not a well-known poem, so I felt kind of proud that I had recognized a clear case of plagiarism. I wrote to the magazine. Unfortunately many other folk seemed to be as equally erudite as I was, and my letter was never published.

Plagiarism, while a problem then, is now rampant. Any and every topic can be accessed easily on the Internet and so students often cut and copy whole chunks of material for their essays. Of course there is software trying to catch all of this such as at www.turnitin.com.

As someone interested in the convolutions of the human mind, I tried to work out whether plagiarism stems from laziness, flattery, or some other possible cause. The fine Canadian poet, George Swede, a man well-versed in the ways of the human mind, was also obliged to similarly explore the plagiarist's mind when he woke up one day to find many (and I mean many) of his haiku appearing on other websites attributed to someone else.

As soon as this case was uncovered, the haiku writers of Canada rose up and girded their loins. Although haijin are usually the most pacific of folk, apparently the manager of one of the sites involved in the plagiarism of George's haiku felt so threatened by the tone of their indignant letters to him that he consulted the police. Actually the righteousness of their cause (the plagiarism of George's haiku) had merely caused them to swell their vocabulary to the use of words such as 'outrageous' and 'unbelievable.'

Before I expand on this incident, I should mention a very clever idea for those of you who actually find your writings plagiarized. In one case that I know of, the person plagiarized sent a bill in for the stolen words, and happily got paid. This example is quoted in www.plagiarismtoday.com. Such a simple and satisfactory solution.

This page: www.poetrylives.com/SimplyHaiku/SHv3n3/ tracks/tracks_v3n3.html tells part of George Swede's story. The other part can be found in a brilliant essay by George in the *Haiku Canada* newsletter, Volume XIX, February 2006, Number 1, (reproduced from *FrogPond*) where George analyzes the mind of the plagiarist. He enters the mind and traces the steps of plagiarism from a person (the plagiarist) reading a haiku and resonating with it; resonating so much that they share it with others because it expresses their thoughts so well. The plagiarist, in George's case, added visuals and music and was so entranced at his creation that he copyrighted the whole effort under his own name. The plagiaristic act was successful and so he proceeded with other haiku. George's plagiarist eventually had all his stolen haiku expunged from the sites that they had appeared on ... but his success over a number of years might leave him vulnerable to try again.

George wrote this wonderful haiku about the whole event:

found: my sunrise haiku
with someone else's name –
this dawn dark

And here are a few of George's wonderful haiku that even I would be tempted to steal:

at the height
of the argument the old couple
pour each other tea

statue in the square
the raised hand of the war hero
fills with snow

over the earth's edge
they all go   the white clouds
and the one sail boat

At a philosophical level, plagiarism brings up the question of originality, which William Inge says is actually undetected plagiarism. Josh Billings supports this point of view by saying that "about the most originality that any writer can hope to achieve honestly is to steal with good judgement", as Will Durant adds "nothing is new except arrangement." Montaigne, who copiously added others' words to his own in his essays, and often took the trouble to rearrange them, excuses himself by saying, "I only quote others to make myself explicit." He usually attributed his quotes, but I am not erudite enough to recognize the many places where he probably didn't. I feel Montaigne has lots in common with Apollodorus, to whom he does attribute this quote, "If all that were not my own were cut out of my works, the paper would be quite blank."

Judicious stealing is the key, I suppose, for musician Peter Townsend, who didn't steal judiciously, complains to an anonymous person "So much of what I am, I got from you. I had no idea how much of it was second-hand." Oh dear! That does seem to leave writers on somewhat shaky ground, maybe we should finish with a good old curse:

Pereant qui ante nos nostra dixerent! – Aelius Donatus

(Perish those who said good things before we did.)

Writers, Realities and Blocks

Several writers boast that they have never experienced writer's block. Some, in fact, don't seem to be able to curb the tapping out of words. As William Pritchard said of John Updike, rather meanly I think, "He must have had an unpublished thought, but you couldn't tell." Most of us, however, from time to time, have what might be recognized as a block of creative energies. This leaves us frustrated and wondering what to do about it. Here is one pattern of behaviour that may work for you. It certainly works for me.

The Writer's Life (at a moment of block)

She loved to read writers on writing;
how they went down to the basement
at 4 a.m. every morning to write,
or shut husband and children out of
their study at 9 a.m., or left
wife and child in order to live
in the wilderness for three months.
And once in their own room, or hut
or cubby-hole, she loved to read
how they slit their wrists before
they could get a word down or
looked out the window all morning
waiting for a poem to break through
the pane. Then she imagined them

with their computer, typewriter,
or yellow pad and pencil at
a well-polished desk and was
enchanted to see a bowl of fresh
anemones sitting there, or a dog
at foot, or cat in lap.
At time of writer's block,
she loved to read about writers writing.

Now every writer knows that there is a cycle of inspiration followed by perspiration, exasperation, exhilaration – and finished with a total wipe out. This wipe out period should not be confused with writer's block. This time, at the end of a large block of writing, is when the field should be left fallow, for the field needs to be rested, manured, green cropped ... to experience a whole slew of enrichments, so that once more it can bring forth a good harvest.

Writer's block is not this. It is a physical inability to put pen to paper, fingertips to computer keys, or quill to parchment. It doesn't feel as though one is drained after a long writing session, it feels as though one has never written before. This feeling pervades even though there may be books and manuscripts to refute it lying on the desk. The blocked writer wonders who wrote them and whether he, or she, will ever do another book again.

Excuses while the writer is blocked often equal excuses for procrastinating ... procrastinating before doing anything: I was going to start, but life got in the way, I'm not sure where to begin it's such a big project, I'm just too old for this game, There are so many good books out on the subject, why am I ... The feeble excuses can swell to outrageous: I'm putting my family life first, I'm waiting for a grant, The right contract hasn't been offered yet, I'm waiting for quiet, I'm waiting for the Muse to strike.

Norman Mailer states categorically that "writer's block is simply a failure of ego," as if a 'failure of ego' is a simple matter. Dean Koontz also states dogmatically, and rather self-righteously, that "I never get writer's block. I've never had it. Writer's block comes from one thing, and one thing only, for every writer, and that is self-doubt." Self-doubt, failure of ego, depression, anxiety, indecision – all these negative words associated with writer's block can only pull the writer deeper into self-blame and guilt. Instead of pinning labels (including the label writer's block) on your chest, why not try to observe the condition detachedly and see what helpful suggestions are offered for removing it.

Neurologists describe the writer's block as a battle between the frontal lobe and the temporal lobe. If the functioning of the temporal lobe of the brain decreases, the condition of hypergraphia (inability to stop writing) comes up. If the frontal lobe is under active, writer's block arises. How to balance the two and call a truce? That the temporal lobes should be in good condition seems to be necessary for the understanding of the meaning of words. The lobes are strongly connected to the limbic system, which governs our emotions and drives. So it does seem that if writer's block has a physical element, then it might possibly be associated with the limbic system, as well as those lobes.

And while we are make suggestions in the physical area, it could be that the winter blues can cause writer's block. If so, Alice W. Flaherty, who helped me with the last paragraph (the errors are mine) suggests you keep a small light box next to your breakfast cereal. If you want to explore the physical aspects of writer's block a little more, Flaherty's book *The Midnight Disease* is to be recommended. She, herself, suffered a couple of bouts of hypergraphia and as she is also a neurologist, became deeply interested in the subject. If you can't get the book locally, her brilliant exposition on hypergraphia and writer's block is at www.susanohanian.org/show_commentary.php?id=186.

Robert Birnbaum has a great interview with her at www.identitytheory.com/interviews/birnbaum141.php. Anyway, I hope the neurologists sort this out soon.

But most writers don't want to explore possible causes of their block, they just want to be unblocked. As Flaherty says, "it didn't matter how I did it [healed the client's writer's block], it still feels great when your thoughts take off."

Before we writers try the many suggestions that are thrust on us by others out there in the world, I think it is a good idea to pause and see if we don't actually have very valid reasons for not writing at this moment. Maybe we actually don't have time to write because we are choosing to give our job and our household full of kids priority. Maybe we need our energy to heal an illness, or maybe our energy needs to be pulled in because we have something we need to grieve about. If none of this applies, then why not look directly at your block and write about it; how it is manifesting and what you think might be its cause. At least you will be writing, and you may surprise yourself by what comes up.

Writer's block is associated with extreme self-criticism, depression and its accompanying lack of drive. I'm not into antidepressants, or, indeed, any kind of drug. They may, however, be indicated as useful for the block, and you should check with your physician about that. Here I can only provide you with some drug-free recommended behaviours that I have found useful:

- Some say, "Wait." Natalie Goldberg puts this so well when she recommends "Wait until you are hungry to say something, until there is an aching in you to speak." There is much to be said for the 'take a break' school. Keats would change into his best clothes and take a walk. Others suggest doing something physical, such as chores, gardening, somersaults.

- A successful recipe I've found is to lower your standards, that is, treat the manuscript as a first draft. That way you'll relax and jot down whatever seems to fit, knowing that you can edit it out later. And while you're relaxed, write down things that may not fit; anything that enters your head, free-associate a topic, brainstorm it. All these actions will oil the mental processes. If you keep your topics in separate files, ideas that come up can be freely distributed throughout the manuscript as they fit.

- And while we are on about lowering standards why not throw the occasional manuscript away. I can hear you draw a horrified breath in, but I mean it. What is so special about what you have written, or rather got stuck in the middle of writing, that the world needs to read it? If you are writing *J'Accuse* I will withdraw this suggestion, otherwise I stand my ground. I have thrown a couple of book-length manuscripts away and extracted a rather nice haiku from another one. It left me free to breathe, and, I might mention, to write freely once more.

- In extremis, start talking and continue until something you say suddenly catches your attention and you get interested – write it down!

- Being rather ornery I find that if I force myself to do another task, the moment I am settled into it, I feel the writing juices filling my muscles. Soon the job I've chosen feels like a straightjacket which I am desperate to get out of. In no time flat I've done the chore and onto the computer. There's nothing like forbidding someone like me to do something.

- Have several projects going at once. I know a well-known non-fiction writer who has three books spinning at the same time as well as commitments for several articles. That way if one seems 'dead' she can always turn to another. You could also try another genre to see whether your ideas might not find it easier to slip out in poetry, rather than prose, or true romance instead of science fiction. If writing in general seems impossible, then make the switch to projects in other areas that interest you – reading all John Le Carré's books in one swoop say, or opening a new flower bed in the garden, or spending more time with your friends, or ...

- Change the method of writing. If you usually write on the computer try a pen and thick yellow pad, or go down to the beach and get a seagull's feather and make a quill pen. This sounds facetious but changing the method of writing, the place of writing or the time of writing, throwing your routine ways of doing things around a bit may just give you the jolt you need. After all writer's block apparently has physical, intellectual and emotional elements to it, so why not attack on all fronts?

- I don't know a cure for perfectionism, but I do know that it is another sure source of writer's block as your expectations for yourself and your actual achievements often part company. Being a rather bright child, and a twin, great things were expected of me, and, until I was forty, I spent the time trying to fulfil those expectations which I had incorporated into my own psyche. At forty, I threw it all over, and while I can't say I have absolutely no regrets, I can say life has been a whole lot easier for me and for surrounding folk. And, it was at that moment, that I really started to write.

- Since drive seems to be the lacking quality at times of block, why not get a mortgage? I don't know why they recommend that writers shouldn't have one, for mine is an ever present goad. Often the raw necessity of meeting the mortgage will overcome the lack of drive to write. If it doesn't, then you are in a bad way, for you will not only be a blocked writer, but also a homeless one.

Whether you leave your desk for a diversion, assuming your brain is collecting its thoughts for you, or whether you tie yourself to your desk and break through your own resistance, there are several things you are advised to definitely not do at time of block. These include beating yourself up, deciding to quit writing forever and setting goals, which, I'm afraid, like New Year's good resolutions, will fade away within a few days.

Does writers' block have anything to do with the way we writers view the world, I wonder? There are as many world views as there are writers, I suspect, so maybe it is something more basic, something involved in the way writers allow themselves, as ordinary people, to be invaded by this writer kind of person, who takes over and pours out words through them.

Writers are often accused of not being able to deal with reality. Of course writers of protest, like Zola, dealt very well with reality, but I suppose it is true that most writers create their own reality because the world around them is almost unbearable. That does not mean that writers' realities are any less real. The following poem was written in response to Colin Haycroft's scathing condemnation of writers.

"A publisher is a specialized form of bank or building society, catering for customers who cannot cope with life and are therefore forced to write about it." – Colin Haycroft

Not Coping

Coping with life!
Of course we can't
cope with life!
Which sane person can?
Can cope with children
on grass mats
sick with AIDS;
the parts of human remains
in Israel, London, New York,
Iraq, Bali ...
distributed on fruit stands,
beaches, street lights,
temples, sidewalks;
the strange things we do
before we can call on the gods,
and the stranger things we do
to folks to whom the gods reply.
How should we cope with pimps,
drug barons, extortionists
and other bullies, and families
who kill each other over breakfast.
We should cope with that!
And with tyrants who shut us away
for years in distant Gulags
and closer internment camps.
The holocaust can barely
be said in the same breath
as "cope" – no sane person
can explain away that one.
That's why the hopeful budding
of cherry trees is so important
to us writers, and early
morning skies before they
get breathed on ...
Those we can cope with.

Wisława Szmborska, my favourite poet, wrote a poem on this very subject, and called it "Reality Demands". In it she states that "This terrifying world is not devoid of charms, of the mornings that make waking up worthwhile," and then she continues to mention items of everyday significance – ice cream men selling to children, orchards blooming, couples dancing on the sunlit decks of yachts. But, and here is the dagger in the poem, these ordinary events are all taking place where there have been battlegrounds of great destruction.

Which is more real, the dying fields, or the small everyday acts of kindness and pleasure? But then, what is reality any way, and don't we each create our own? As Edward Albee says, "Good writers define reality; bad ones merely restate it." I remember the artist, Louis Nevelson, saying that she created her own reality because the one outside wasn't so great, or words to that effect, although she understood that "what we call reality is an agreement that people have arrived at to make life more liveable." And maybe writers being out of touch with reality causes less of a problem than say presidents, or lawyers, being out of touch. There is an Islamic claim that 38% of Americans are out of touch with reality (a trifle low, I would have thought). At other times and places, Hollywood, endocrinologists, and the Miss America Pageant have also been so accused. For myself, I would like to get a button (put out by NancyButtons, I believe) that says "I don't mind being in touch with reality so long as I don't have to live there."

Now back to writer's block for a moment, for the time when writers and reality really clash and the writer's block looms large is often after their first book is published, or even just after their first byline appears in a magazine. The budding writer immediately assumes that a certain curve is about to happen in their career and unhelpful friends will boost this feeling by asking when the writer's next writing is to appear.

When the curve droops, the contracts don't arrive and reality doesn't match expectations, that is the moment for self-flagellation to begin and in its wake, the dreaded writer's block. All I can say about this is that if it is happening to you, please accept what reality is offering you, drop your expectations and write for the love of it. If the love isn't there, then go drive a taxi for a bit, or do something helpful for others. If you remain blocked, and if your ego is solidly tied to your success in writing, then find some other way to boost your esteem. If it isn't, then, when you are ready to write, you will write. I'm talking to myself again, aren't I. Who else will take my advice?

Read My Lips

Many writers are so terrified of reading in public that they consider getting surrogate readers to do it for them. Others, equally nervous, have suggested starting by reading to children, because they are so forgiving. I wonder where they got hold of that idea. The books I'm writing now are not directed at a juvenile audience, but when I did read one of my juvenile titles to a class, they nitpicked it to pieces on points such as whether socks stayed the same colour throughout the story, and were indignant because the tale didn't have a completely happy ending ... no, stay with an adult audience if you can. Some anonymous writer on the web overcomes their fears of reading their works in public, to some extent, by imagining their audience "naked and Republican." This would be a difficult thing for me to do, although, while I am struggling with the image, my reading time would certainly be cut into. Still other writers suggest that if you really push yourself and start reading in non-traditional places, such as planes and streetcars and supermarkets, that any audience after that will seem almost relaxing. So if your knees tremble at the thought of folks sitting in rows in front of you, clinging on your lips, perhaps *extreme* reading is for you.

Some writers, rather pompously I feel, believe that reading in public helps the audience understand the artistic process and that is why writers should do it. I simply feel I owe it to my publisher for the months she has devoted to my writing during editing, and the cash she has put out to publish and promote my books. Readings in public bring you, and your book, to the attention of the book-buying public and, it is hoped, increases interest in your work; with the interest to be followed by a purchase. Shoppers like to sample the goods before they buy. I once heard of a publisher who took on an unknown poet, only to find, after his book had been published, that he refused to appear in public. They sold six copies of the print run which even for poetry is low.

Unlike the writers above, I love reading in public. The first laugh I can raise hooks me, even if the audience is not totally likewise hooked. I've learned that self-deprecation goes over well and, by that, I do not mean apologising at the beginning of a reading somewhat along the lines that "really my poetry isn't up to much, but I did manage, by scrambling, to find a few humble verse that might very well have some appeal to you." Don't laugh. I can't tell you how many writers start their readings in this way. When being self-deprecating in public, you actually need to feel quite good about yourself and your writing, to be able to point up your foibles. You are, after all, human, and probably share most of your short comings with the audience, who are therefore laughing with you, and not at you. I was at a wedding recently and found that the folks who did the toasts laughed uproariously at their own jokes, often before their audience did, or, indeed, sometimes without the audience joining them. I tend to keep a rather straight face after reading an amusing bit, or, at the most, give a rather sweet, but slightly sad smile.

I remember reading Kiran Nagarkar's account of the moment he got hooked on audience applause, and how, after that, "my family and friends had a difficult time preventing me from buying my own air-tickets to international literary festivals in Iceland, Siberia and the Galapagos Islands, all so I could appear uninvited on the podium, shoving the scheduled author aside, to read from my own work." Now that's attitude.

I love small audiences (not too small) and I love to know that they have connected with me either with laughter, or with the movement of hand and tissue to eye. I am coming to understand that reading in public is an art that can be learned, and so I jotted down some pointers for those of you who are thinking of pursuing the profession of writer, and with it, the necessary public readings.

Firstly I rehearse like mad. I've discovered that appearing spontaneous takes an awful lot of rehearsing. I time myself when practising, so that I give the organizer and the audience exactly what they expect. It is better to run slightly under the allotted time, than over it, leaving the audience, one hopes, panting for more. I remember an incident where a poet got carried away on his own poem. When he had entered stanza nine, we felt for sure it would end at ten. It didn't. The nervous emcee sidled up to the poet and whispered to him that he had exceeded his time. The poet lashed around with a loud "Shut-up! Don't ever do that again!" and proceeded until the poem ended at stanza 24.

Read in front of the mirror when you are practicing, for it is odd how unaware we are of nervous habits such as twisting your hair, scratching your head, or tapping on your nose. Hands should clutch the script, or the lectern, or hang gracefully at your sides. We want the audience to concentrate on our words and movements distract. I was at a house-concert the other week where the performer knocked his knees together several times at certain ill-defined moments in his performance. I tried to find a pattern, a reason, but I couldn't, and so the performance went on with my ears distracted by my eyes on those knees.

If I am not given limits, I usually keep my readings to 20 minutes. One page of prose usually takes two minutes to read. If I'm reading to an unknown audience, I try to vary the topics of the poems in sets. For example I might start with poems on writing, after all that is why we are all gathered together in this back room of the library. Then I might follow with poems on death (a favourite topic of mine), iconoclastic attempts, relationships (always a popular area for linking to the audience) and finish up with a couple of poems that will either leave them laughing, or crying. Yes, I like to start with having the audience in laughter and finish by having them crying (or vice versa) but either way, I have a poem with a strong impact at the beginning and end of the reading. For family readings, such as on Family Literacy Days, I prepare a general selection of poems that keep away from the genital area.

If I know something about the venue, I try to match the material – local gossipy poems that my islanders are in on for a hometown launch; more protest and relationship poems for city readings; and heartstring pluckers for the small town libraries, which are my favourite places to read. My publisher pronounced that I could "Wow" any audience that didn't have body piercings, and I am sticking to her advice. In case I am asked, I have also prepared a reading of poems solely on the topic of writing, one with the theme of love, and one on gardening. The latter is great for garden club presentations, for I have discovered that reading in places where it is unconventional for writers to read sells copies just as well as at poetry cafes.

When I read, I want the same buzz of excitement that I had when I first wrote the piece. If I find half a page has gone by and I've no idea what I've read, I cut that section from my next presentation. If I'm too bored to be involved in what I've just read, how can I expect the audience to stay enchanted?

If you have a threatening cold, or your nervousness brings on a croak, make sure you have bottled water with you, and cough drops. My husband complains that my cheek bulges on one side during my readings, but better bulge than cracked voice, and while we are on the subject of comfort, make sure your clothes are comfortable and don't distract you physically. A friend of mine grabbed a new pair of panty hose before one reading, only to discover they were control top and that the top that was the controlling factor cut into her stomach and, because the stomach was attached to the rest of her, cut into her breath control.

I wear interesting clothes, not because the audience has come to see what I am wearing, but because it is part of the show (and one can't pretend that showmanship isn't part of sales, even of delicate poetry book sales) and because of that, I respect the audience down to wearing fresh underwear and clean socks. I have, myself, organized poetry readings where poets in grubby jeans fish into their pockets to drag out a dirty piece of paper into which they proceed to whisper. They neither respect that the audience has got off of its respective couches to come out to hear them, often paying an entrance fee, nor, I think, do they respect themselves, or their writing. I consider only my audience and my respect for poetry – they are both worth clean clothes, and poems written on crisp, clean paper, and a good strong voice so that the listeners don't have to strain forward in their seats to hear what I have to tell them. And while we are talking about strong voices, if you insist on accompanying yourself on a guitar, make sure you have a mike; older people in the audience have trouble with a double lot of sounds coming at them. Oh, by the way, a last word on clothes. I've found successful poets tend to wear large scarves that can be thrown around the body, or draped dramatically on the floor. It takes a bit of practice to handle a scarf, but it's worth it.

A thing I find really distressing at readings is a disorganized writer who has the poetry sequence scribbled on a small card and then has to dig through the book they are reading from, in order to find the first poem. Of course there needs to be pauses between poems, or sections of writing, so that the audience knows when the reader has finished one, and when the next is about to begin. The pause, however, should be stillness, and not consist of pages being crackled and the sound of papers scattering around at the writer's feet. The writer could smooth things along by having marked the pages from which he, or she, is going to read and by having written the number sequence on the notes so that they merely have to look for 1, 2, 3, etc. as they proceed with their reading. I won't even discuss writers who change their mind about their choice of reading, in public, with the subsequent lengthy hiatus.

Because I am older, with weakening vision and memory, I type the whole presentation out in 16 point type, including the segues between the poems. That way I can read the poem and not lose track of where I'm at, or get diverted by my segues and find myself at the end of the universe, instead of at the beginning of the next poem. Having a script in large print also allows me to glance up frequently at the audience.

The few times I have felt a little nervous before a reading have been when I was ill-prepared, had doubts about the suitability of my selection of poetry for the reading, or was concentrating too much on me, me, me, instead of them, them, them.

Assuming you have floated through the reading successfully, consider allowing time for questions after your reading. You may think that your public wants to know about you and the sort of person you are and why you write that kind of writing, and often that is true. A friend of mine, a comparatively well-known writer, went on a promotion tour of his new book along with a couple of other men. The sales from the readings were paltry ... one book here, maybe two there. At the last reading of the series, the by now fed-up writers decided to sit on the stage and talk about themselves, the way they work, and their lives. The audience rose to their feet in hordes and bought.

On the other hand, to be honest, the questions after a reading usually start with "How do I get my children's story, that my grandchildren love so much, published?" Sometimes some members of the audience are so busy concentrating on the question they urgently need answering, that they haven't heard that it has already been asked, and answered. In this case, my advice is to give them full attention and respond as if you, too, had not already heard, and answered, the question. I really care that these folks have taken the trouble to come to listen to me and try to treat them with respect and full attention. I will often wander into the audience to stand by the questioner in order to make eye contact and, because I am getting deafer by the year, ear contact.

I try to feel out the audience's needs and make them as happy as possible. I remember being horrified at Mordecai Richler responding with a blunt, "No" when asked to repeat an amusing story that a woman in the audience had heard him tell elsewhere and that she thought the fans might enjoy. He lost a few over that, I imagine.

Selling books after a reading is often assisted by the organizer. I remember one library reading where the enthusiastic chief librarian, after he had thanked me, declared "Now Naomi didn't leave her little island just to read to you. She'll want you to look at her books and buy, so come on up and do just that." And they did, to my crimson-faced amazement. On the other hand look out for fond parents pushing their genius child ahead of them towards your book table and announcing loudly that this prodigious infant has a book they would like you to read ... right now! If you are doing the selling yourself, (and you may very well have to) remember the cash box and a float. A Dixie cup will substitute for a cash box, but for a float there is no substitute. Oh! I almost forgot, bring a pen for that autographing.

Be prepared for anything – having to set out the chairs yourself, being presented with a music stand that is too frail to hold even a slim book of poems, an audience of only three people (all of whom have come in out of the rain), an introducer who hasn't checked on some of the more relevant facts of your life, or the reality that the organizer and you did not seem to have coincided on the date you thought you had mutually agreed on. It is all in the interest of promoting writers and writing, so sigh, don't complain, and arrange those chairs yourself.

Recently at the launch of a new book, the venue became overcrowded and I found myself calling out and pointing wildly towards the odd spare chair that might not have been noticed. A writer in the audience walked over to me and pointed out that it is not dignified for the presenter to act as usher. I blushed, but as I had only wanted to speed up the seating process so that the reading could start, I didn't feel too abashed.

For a wonderfully amusing description of a poetry reading do check out Wisława Szymborska's great poem, *Poetry Reading*. It is in her book *Poems New and Collected.*

To sum up the gains from reading your writing in public – you keep your publisher happy, you test what works and what doesn't work for your audience, you keep your publisher happy, you gather a supportive group of readers, you keep your publisher happy, you might get a modest honorarium, you keep your publisher happy.

The Problem with Publishers

As I quoted in *Late Bloomer: On Writing Later in Life,* "Submitted in haste, returned at leisure." With these words, Oliver Herford defined manuscript submission bluntly and truly. Why won't publishers phone in joy at receiving our fabulous manuscripts, or, at the very least respond to our frantic emails? I'm sure there is a good answer to these questions we ask.

But, hold your horses, let's start at the beginning, for before we can complain about a publisher, we have to find one. Only then can we progress to the complaints department.

For the beginning writer, unless you have a book of exceptional excellence (and most think they do), I recommend a small to medium-size publisher for querying. There are still a number of publishing houses of this size who manage to continue year after year making a modest living and promoting a number of fresh writers. The editors can give you full attention as there are rarely more than eight books seeing print under the firm's name in a year. They are more likely to give you the care and encouragement that you crave, even if they may not be able to get you a review in the big dailies.

Patrick Dennis told of one of his experiences with submitting a book: "It circulated for five years, through the halls of fifteen publishers, and finally ended up with the Vanguard Press, which, as you can see, is rather deep in the alphabet."

Perhaps I should start by telling how I got my present publisher for whom this is the third book I am writing in almost as many years. I consider the odds when submitting to a publisher. If the publisher does four books a year and gets 1,000 submissions, then I consider my odds poor. If, however, the publishing house carries other books in the genre I am submitting and the odds are reasonable, I go for it. I don't need to tell you that there is no point in submitting a book on horse grooming to a publisher who specializes in art history, though you'd be amazed at how many people do similar mindless submissions. In the case of my submission to Wolsak and Wynn, I saw that it was a modest firm, which specialized in Canadian poets and had won several awards for their books. Despite the fact I knew nobody in the firm and knew nothing about Wolsak and Wynn except what Google and their website revealed I thought my odds of acceptance were still reasonable.

I sent, I think, about a dozen poems to Wolsak and Wynn by snail mail. Several months passed and during that period I fussed with other things. One day I got an email from them indicating that they really liked one of the poems that I had submitted. They gave its name, and indicated that they wished to see more. I was triumphant and danced around the computer until I realized that the poem they had mentioned was not only not among the ones that I had sent them, but was, unfortunately, not mine at all. I immediately replied, "I have never been so happy and unhappy at the same time." Maybe I put an ! after time, and maybe not, for although I was disappointed, I was not indignant. They replied apologising (an act that omened well, for publishers are not known for this) and named a poem I had sent. They asked me to send another 60, or so, which I did.

And there is the first bit of advice I'd like to give – don't submit one poem, with no backup, or even one novel without future novels in the works. Publishers are going to invest in you and they like to know that a) you are industrious, and b) that you are not a one shot deal. And so the story finished happily for I got a contract, and two more followed.

Some years before, with my first contract with another publishing house, for a large run (10,000 in paperback, and 2,000 hardback), my anxiety and paranoia ran rampant. Gathering the pennies from my money jar, I booked an appointment with a lawyer who specialized in "literary" law. Expecting a learned, mature figure, I was somewhat dismayed to find a willowy young thing (yes, I know that's ageism, but somewhat reversed from my usual experience), sitting on the far side of a large desk. She took the contract and proceeded to read it slowly and loudly (something I could have done equally well, and probably with more expression). She then declared the session finished. I was so bemused that I couldn't remember the one, or two, small points she may have asided during the reading. Outside her room, I stared at my empty notepad and sullenly received the instant invoice from her secretary for $200. And that is why poets starve and lawyers can afford to buy my husband's sculpture.

As it turned out, that publisher, who is a wonderful person, and with whom I became rather friendly, told me that the contract I had received from them was drawn up years ago and she had no idea what was in it. She published the book, her editor edited it, her publicist publicized it and we could have done it all with a handshake!

Here's a poem about a publishing proposal I made. It is dedicated to a publisher who was not as dedicated to haiku as I am:

Sex after 70

I sit across
from my publisher
who cuddles his coffee
and explodes with "What!"
"I'm writing a book on haiku,"
I repeat calmly.
"On haiku!" his face red.
"Why can't you write
something people want to read
like 'fishing on the west coast?'"
"Or sex after 70," I counter.
"Yes, sex after 70,"
his eyes switch from
exasperated to hopeful,
"Now there's a promising title!"
We both fall silent.
I imagine he is weighing up
the odds of me being informed
on the subject, while I
do a quick survey of
a possible table of contents.
Sex and osteoarthritis –
the joints locking
in positions unheard of
in the Kama Sutra.
Choices – orgasm or muscle cramp;
whether to allow myself
the pleasure of orgasm
or go into the pain
of a concurrent foot cramp.
Whether to focus on the vagina
and the blissful dissolving
or the foot and get that spasm
dealt with and those
toes straightened out.
Decisions, decisions and
before I know it I am
thinking of nouns ...

those nouns of haiku
and how each noun
condenses a universe
and packs a wallop
and how two, or three nouns
together, if carefully chosen,
can tumble you into the void
and to universes beyond,
and how the pause, the pause
at the 5th or 12th syllable
opens so many possibilities
to dwarf all orgasms, or cramps
come to that, and transform
dark crows on bare branches
into cockatoos on plum blossom.
"I'm writing the book on haiku,"
I firmly address my publisher
across the steam of his coffee.
he sighs, takes a sip and asks,
"When's the first draft ready?"

Once the contract is signed, then comes the editing. Well the editing may not come for some months/years later, depending on when you have been slotted into the publisher's publishing schedule. Of course, sooner is better than later, but that is not up to you. If the editing begins too far after the contract, the writer has lost all interest in the book and has to spend feverish days trying to drum up enthusiasm while his or her brain is asking "Did I ever write this wretched stuff, and, if I did, why did I?"

Editing may not be an agreeable process to the novice writer who cherishes each of their words as if they were enthroned on silk in Topkapi. Remember Churchill's words on criticism, "Criticism may not be agreeable, but it's necessary. It fulfils the same function as pain in the human body. It calls attention to an unhealthy state of things." Whatever you thought of his politics, you can't deny he was a fine writer. Many think he should have stuck to that profession.

While my editing for this present book began fairly soon after I'd received my contract, still my mind had moved elsewhere and I found myself dialoguing myself – "I'm supposed to make all these changes!" "Yes, you are." "I'm too tired!" "Well, you'd better cut that out and get moving." "If I make these changes, I'll have to change the whole book." "Well who else will make the changes, you wrote the manuscript, didn't you?" "I suppose I'd better take a look then." "Yes, you had." Some time later ... "Wow! I love what I'm doing. My editor's suggestions are great. She really has a vision for me. I'm actually having fun." This was my actual interior dialogue and illustrates how I got caught up in the great creative process that is called editing with a good editor.

So, before I expound on the 'problem with publishers' I should state a disclaimer immediately. My present publishers, and my publishers of the last few years have all been more than supportive. With them, discussions have remained discussions and suggestions have been carefully and thoughtfully considered on both our sides and, to my amazement, emails have been replied to pronto.

But I have given my share of grumbles as well, for I, to my horror and surprise, have had publishers change so many words in a book that the story came out totally differently to the one I had submitted. I have also had my title changed, and had little recourse since the book was already at the printers. I did not have Graham Greene's fame and subsequent strong position when it came to publishers. When receiving the cable from an American publisher considering his manuscript *Travels with my Aunt* which said "Terrific book, but we'll have to change the title," Mr. Greene replied, "No need to change the title. Easier to change the publisher." Ah! one of those repartees one wished was on the edge of the tongue when needed.

S. J. Perelman hints at what can happen next (with an edge of bitter experience one suspects); "Publishers regard writers as vain, petty, juvenile and thoroughly impossible ... so there's no use in attempting to be reasonable with them, or trying to prove that you, as a writer, are a person of dignity who's merely interested in their merchandising your work, a job they frequently aren't equipped to do by any business standards." Yes, zero promotion is the common complaint of many writers, which surprises me, for how is the publisher (at least in Canada) going to make a profit from the book apart from the grant he or she has received to publish it ... or maybe that's enough?

Authors dream of a fully-evolved marketing plan. Publishers, I suppose dream of one or two titles a year being best-sellers (probably not yours). With the ten biggest publishing houses claiming 88.4% of book sales (50% probably taken up by the Harry Potter series and *The Da Vinci Code*), where does the small publisher (and the smaller author) stand? Have a little compassion for publishers. So, my advice is to be thankful you have any kind of a contract and plan an extensive sales trip yourself. As the little red hen in the children's story declared, "Then I'll do it myself," and she did.

I speak with writers who have had the experience of arriving at a small town bookstore to find no posters have been posted, that the local press, radio and TV know nothing about them and that they are condemned to sit at a card table in the mall, outside the bookstore, and talk to shoppers about their beloved book; shoppers who are on their way to buy running shoes, or vacuum bags, or batteries. Recently I was told of a writer whose publisher did all the necessary postering and publicizing for a book launch, but who hadn't known that two other book launches had been slated for the same evening, in the same small town. Three audience members turned up, one of whom, a street person, finding the warmth of the library congenial, took off his shoes and examined his toes carefully during the reading.

I vowed at the time when I started reading in public to promote my books, that even if I only had an audience of one, I would sound out their needs, and give them my full attention. I have managed to convince myself that however many people turn up to my reading it is going to be the correct number for me at that moment, and I should accept it as such. In this way I am never disappointed with my audiences, which have ranged from standing-room-only crowds, to the one time, when only one person did turn up, although a dozen had booked in to hear me read. I had a great discussion with my solo audience about where she was at, and what she could do with her writing, for after all that is what most people want to know when you think they have actually come to hear you read. She bought copiously at the end of our session, so it seems that we were both satisfied.

My favourite place for launching my books is at Pages Marina on the little island on which I live. One of the owners had been a librarian and she held literary court in her beautiful waterfront living room and sold hundreds of books for island authors. She and her husband are now retired, but Phyllis and Ted Reeve will be on the gratitude list of all the writers who have lived for any length of time on Gabriola. Their daughter, Gloria and her husband, Ken, have taken over and luckily for us are carrying on in their parents' tradition. It's great to launch a book when you know most everyone in the packed room and they are forgiving and receptive; one of the advantages of island living for me.

By the way, if you are hoping to have a children's book published, unless you are an amazing illustrator, I should tell you that children's publishers like to match their authors with their own stable of illustrators. They think they are good matchmakers, and often they are, but to see your fine book ruined with illustrations that you loathe leaves you feeling helpless and tragic. Believe me.

Noelle Allen, my publisher, asked me whether a publisher was a necessary evil, a business partner, or an artistic supporter. I qualified each of her options with a "Yes, but." Yes, a publisher is necessary, but not necessarily evil. The alternative is a pile of poorly edited, self-published books in your attic. Yes, the publisher is a business partner, but the author is the one more likely to go broke. Yes, the publisher should be an artistic supporter, but more specifically, *my* artistic supporter.

My idea about the way the publishing process should be is that the publisher shouldn't be a tyrant, nor should the author. Both publisher and author (and editor) want to see a successful book, a book to which everyone is proud they have contributed. Acknowledgments by the author to the team's input in the front pages of the book should not be perfunctory and should ring sincerely.

Authors usually bond with their editors, not their publishers. For my poetry book, *Segues,* I was lucky to have my editor and publisher in one person, and a very sympathetic one too. For *Late Bloomer: On Writing Later in Life* I had a lengthy, but creative and entirely satisfactory editing period with the same company's other editor who has now become the publisher. So, I'd like to repeat my disclaimer that I embedded halfway through this chapter and, please mark, I feel indulged at the moment, and am not always whining.

Parts
of the
Book

Book Jackets

I have achieved the distinction of being asked to write a book jacket blurb. It is for a book of haiku. I prepared myself by studying blurbs on a variety of book jackets. They are by distinguished people, which leads me to rather cynically wonder if the sales of the book doesn't somehow depend on the importance of the person offering the blurb. The blurbs are clever, witty, profound. Most of them don't seem to have too much to do with the book contents though, and I wondered to myself how many pages of the manuscript one needs to read before the book jacket blurb is considered valid or relevant?

I, not being very famous, want desperately to be considered wise, witty or at least clever. I speed read the manuscript submitted to me for blurb. Just how many haiku can you read and absorb and extrapolate from at one sitting, I wonder. When as many as I could possibly absorb were lodged inside my brain, I commanded myself "Write! Just write!" And lo and behold, I did just that:

"XX is a true seer, in that his haiku, deceptively simple, speaking of everyday things, see deeply into the essence of all things. His thorough understanding of the haiku form allows him to style them after Bashō, Buson, Shiki ... but all the while it is XX's wit, compassion and clear-seeing that shine through"

The publisher pronounced it excellent and I gave myself points for creative writing.

Blurbs sit on the back of book jackets, and although the book jacket has been around since the 1830s it wasn't until the 1930s that its function changed from just protecting the book to protecting and advertising the book. Jacket as protection was an inadequate idea anyway. Paul Collins points out so rightly that if a book is stored upright, as it usually is, then the dust jacket does not protect the part of the book that is exposed to dust. But back to jackets as advertising. Books these days try to outdo each other in colour, design, holographic art, cute flaps that open to disclose ... the author's face ... and, of course blurbs. Paul Collins' take on jacket design is that, "if a book cover has raised lettering, metallic lettering, or raised metallic lettering, then it is telling the reader: 'Hello. I am an easy-to-read work on espionage, romance, a celebrity, and/or murder.'" He adds, "To readers who do not care about such things, this lettering tells them: 'Hello. I am crap.'" You can read his fine analysis of book covers in his book about the book-selling town of Hay-on-Wye, *Sixpence House*.

While the book cover has to persuade the purchaser to pick the book up, the back-cover blurb should seal the deal. The word "blurb" came from a comic character drawn by Gelett Burgess who he called Miss Belinda Blurb. She was a satire on all lavish illustrations of femme fatale or of damsels in distress that seemed to grace book jackets at that time (in 1907). Burgess later defined 'blurb' as "1) a flamboyant advertisement, an inspired testimonial. 2) Fulsome praise; a sound like a publisher."

These days blurbs seem to be viewed as slightly tainted, as though nepotism is always involved. Certainly the relationship between the blurb writer and the author can be questioned, but why couldn't it, as in my case, be someone writing about someone else's haiku that they truly admire. The fact that we both belong to Haiku Canada, and, indeed to the western wing –

pacifikana – is not really relevant. The author knows a lot about haiku and he knows I know a bit, or at least I know a good one when I read one, so why shouldn't he ask me? The connection does not have to be nefarious.

Among the blurbs I used for my book of poetry, *Segues,* was one from a writer who didn't know me at all. It was the critique I received from one of the manuscript's readers before I got my contract. It had a certain integrity. Sure it praised the poems, but it did something else too, that blurbs don't usually do, because this reader wasn't writing a blurb, he was giving a frank evaluation of a manuscript for which the publisher would have to put up funds in order to publish and promote. That's what gave it integrity.

Richard Harrison, a fine poet, wrote of *Segues:*

"I loved this poetry. This is someone who's seen life, knows it pulls no punches, and who can still laugh like a child running down a hill. I can hear her voice. I can hear her."

That blurb changed how I viewed myself. Blurbs can do that too.

By the way, I was just introduced to a great solution if you cannot count a well-known person among your possible blurbists, and that is to use a quote from a famous person. It won't be about your book, of course, but it may fit the target very well and people, being usually careless, won't notice that it isn't a direct blurb. Of course the best-informed blurbs are from people who have actually read the book, but which blurbists have time to do that these days? Back blurbs often come from promotional material that the blurbist glances through, so, in a way, publishers write their own blurbs.

Recently the back cover seems to be concentrating on direct sales, with often a single piece of stunning text, or a very good reason to buy the book, such as, "Seven Ways this Book will Change your Marriage," or, "Retire at 30!" While the book may only spend 25% of its life with its back cover uppermost, actually 40% of the time a potential buyer looks at a book he or she will be looking at the back cover, or so I'm told.

If it's not blurbs people complain about, it is the photo of the author on the inside flap of the book jacket. And I often complain too, for it's usually showing the best profile, if there is one, or, if there isn't, a hat casts a heavy shade over the worst facial features. The authors are always smiling ... why are they smiling? Did they get a big advance?

Doctors on Book Jackets

Why are they smiling
so complacently those
doctors on book jackets?
Asking us to trust them
at least this time, and that
we will be well rewarded, but,
as Charlie Brown does, when Lucy
holds the ball for him to kick,
we, too, wonder whether they won't fail
us again, yet once more, in spite of
their smiles on book jackets.

When people speak of book jackets, they rarely mention the spine, and yet it is the spine they will, more or less, be confronted with in any bookstore (unless the publisher has paid thousands of dollars to have the books piled, front face up, at the front of the store). In the past the manuscript owner would take his sheath of printed papers to the binder and often the binding would match other books in his library

– perhaps red leather embossed with gold lettering. The spine had no writing on it since the book was shelved with the spine inwards. It wasn't until the 16th century that spines began to look like we see them today. You may not have noticed, but spines, when not printed horizontally (if the book is large enough) are printed from top to bottom in North America and vice versa in Europe. The North Americans say the spine is more easily read when the book is face up, if it is printed top to bottom, the other school says that if the book is face up, you don't need the information on the spine. It all sounds a little like something Jonathan Swift would have written! As space is limited on the spine, capital letters are recommended. Although the spine usually has the title, author's and publisher's name, the cover art work may well run right across it. In that case, the letters should be bold enough to be read at five feet away, or at least at arm's length.

As I said, publishers pay large sums to have their books stacked at the front of giant bookstore chains. For the run-of-the-mill book, the spine is usually all that shows to the buying public. About this, I have a moment of true confession, for, in the infancy of my writing life, I would from time to time, pop into the nearest store and rearrange my books slightly, making sure I had at least a few front covers exposed. Recently I met a complete stranger while awaiting the Nanaimo ferry, and, as is the wont among islanders, I started up a conversation. It turned out she had a high federal government position, but was on the verge of retiring. We discussed writing and books and I spurted out the above confession to her, as one often finds oneself confessing odd things to total strangers. She laughed, and said she had lots of time on her hands and she actually wrote down a number of my titles and offered to pop into the Vancouver stores and do a little adjusting for me.

Book covers can just be type on a solid colour, type with design, or type that suggests the mood, or content, such as oriental-style type for a samurai novel. Pictures can be added suggesting the atmosphere of the book, or even showing the characters at a crisis moment. Whatever the cover, the artist usually competes with the commercial publicity department of the publishing house. The artist wants it beautiful and outstanding, the sales department just wants it to stand out. Bookstores add their two-halfpence by wanting the design of the cover to reflect exactly what's in the book, and the age range of the reader. Kindergarten books, they feel, should be primary colours and cartoon figures. Chick-lit can be cartoon also, but should definitely be up-beat and sexy. Books with just a solid colour cover, but with strong title type can be very compelling, and the subtleties of the type can perhaps act subliminally on your buying resistance.

Whichever way you look at it, a book jacket should reflect the mood of the book, and, if the mood reflects your own at the moment, you will pick it up. As to colour, white, or black are most dramatic, but kids, as bookstore owners claim above, like primary colours. I have recently done a series of chapbooks of my poetry. Each chapbook covered a certain topic. I chose the colours like this: for the book on *Writing*, I chose the yellow of a standard pencil, for *Gardening*, obviously green, for a book on *Getting you Writing*, I chose peach (but it came out a rather shocking pink) and on *Loving*, what else could it be but red? My next book was on ageing (appropriately called *Ageing*) and I was thinking that purple would be a cliché, but that grey would be too depressing. Although the subjects of sickness, old age and death are sometimes depressing, my poems are infinitely cheerful, or, at least, cynical, so I compromised by using a periwinkle blue.

For the cover of the chapbook on *Writing*, I suddenly seized a brush and randomly painted strokes across the solid yellow cover. When I looked at them closely, there was the word "Zen" both on the front and on the back, albeit rather stylized. The reason that was interesting to me is that I am a sucker for Zen-like covers – a single blade of grass, a reflecting pool, patterns in the sand ... ah I would buy books with covers like that without even glancing at their contents.

Usually the writer and the cover designer are kept well apart by the publisher, but, if you are both the writer and the designer, you at least have the advantage of knowing what the book is all about. When it comes to designing the cover yourself, as I did with my chapbooks, you can always play it safe with a simple title at the top and author's name at the bottom, or vice versa if you're feeling very cocky about yourself. If you have Photoshop, Illustrator, Paintshop or Freehand, and know how to use them, you might break lose and make the cover an extravaganza. Of course in the process, you may very well have lost the essence of the story you had meant to capture. Although your goal may not be to create a masterpiece, but to actually sell the book, why not have a good time while you're at it? But be warned, small publishers, and definitely self-publishers, seem to spend far too much on the cover and this must certainly cut into their profits.

Cover-designer, Lewis Agrell, is firmly against self-publishers designing their own covers. Agrell pleads, "You wouldn't rewire your house yourself; you'd hire a professional electrician. The same goes for book cover design. Hire a professional." But then he's a book designer, isn't he?

As a rather depressing postscript: blurb, or photo, or whatever hysteria manifests on the book jacket, the truth seems to be that, these days, unless the book is a prize winner, or shoots to the top ten of *The New York Time's* booklist, or is chosen by Oprah, it is likely to be buried, unmourned, in the remainder box, within, let's say, six weeks of its launch party.

Book Dedications

Feeling guilty that I had not read Montaigne's essays, although I had quoted from him in my introduction to this book, I have just spent a happy few days doing so. The introduction to his essays, by J.M.Cohen, was 11 pages long and so not too intimidating. It provided a history and a setting for the essays and I found it enormously helpful. Most people appear not to read introductions, for if commenting on them, they express surprise that the introduction was so helpful, as I did, or preface their comments with, "I am not one who usually reads forwards and introductions." Shakti Babalon complains bitterly about *The Bardo Thodol* that it has "more footnotes than text, but almost half the book is a series of forwards and introductions." Having sampled this book, which was fashionable to read in the 70s, I can also remember searching, almost in vain, for some text in order to grasp the most important instructions, that I apparently needed 30 years ago, on how to die and be reborn properly. One reader complained of the 100 pages of forwards and introductions to the 700 page *The Worst Journey in the World* by Apsley Cherry-Gerrard. Whether it actually was the worst journey in the world I don't know, because I never read the book, but it certainly sounds like the worst journey into a book.

Apparently in the academic world forwards and introductions are taken seriously, and are often listed in the author's bibliography, as in the case of Theodore Hesburgh. This is a gentleman of whom I have never heard until now, and I am amazed at the long list of introductions and forwards he has written for other people's books. I wonder whether one could make a living by just writing these?

On the whole, most people want to get into the plot, or substance, of the book as quickly as possible, so they skip the beginning bits. I usually do too, but there is one item before the book starts in dead earnest that I never skip, and that is the dedication. In fact I have become quite rigid, in that I will not read a book where the author doesn't dedicate it to "the love of my life" or at least to the author's dog. I feel that writers should have a muse who inspires, and not just write for the hell of it, or because they want to. Gratitude to the universe, or at least to someone in it, is obligatory for me. It warms me a little to the author, before I've even read a word, and predisposes me a little more kindly towards them.

While choice of title can be, and often is, usurped by the publisher, the dedication has to be written by the author. When reading a dedication, I sometimes wonder whether the dedication is connected to the book contents, that is, was the dedicatee part of the love story told, the experiments done, the walks taken within the book, or is it just the duty dedication that the world has come to expect?

Dedications, of course, began by necessity, the necessity of praising the patron who was funding the book, or whose patronage would further its sales. Without the patron, the writer would be shivering over a single candle in her, or his attic. Jane Austen reluctantly dedicated *Emma* to the Prince Regent; so reluctantly that the publisher had to spruce it up by adding a little more flattery. The King James Bible's dedication begins "To the most high and mighty Prince, King James 1 of England" putting him nearly on the level of his God.

Nineteenth century dedications tended to be gushing, sentimental and lengthy. These days dedications seem to fall into three categories: long ones that almost blend into acknowledgements so urgently does the author want not to leave anyone unmentioned; one-liners usually to wives, husbands or lovers (sometimes one and the same), and abrupt ones consisting of merely the name, or the relationship – "to mother."

The one-liners, when not enigmatic still seem to smack of sentiment and cliché – "To X who is always there for me," To Y, my most precious," "To Z who never doubted my dreams," and, of course to parents being "the reason I am here today." A review of the *Bloomsbury Dictionary of Dedications,* describes it as, "a catalogue of favourite aunts, perfect spouses and the profoundest platitudes. Dedications really do bring out the worst in authors."

I love gossip, and so it is the enigmatic dedications that stir up my interest. Why is he dedicating this book to her, when he dedicated the previous one to another? What's the story there? Relationships do change, I know, as in the case of Graham Greene who dedicated *Journey without Maps* to his wife, and when love grew cold, changed it in later editions to 'my cousin, Barbara Strachwitz.' Saul Bellow changed wives (and dedications) four times, five wives in all. He died after using the fifth dedication, so Janis Freedland became his final dedicatee. He used the words, "The star without whom I could not navigate," but navigate the Styx he did, and without her.

When it comes to dedications to loves, the French humorist Alphonse Allais seems to have found a good generic one, "To the only woman I love, and who knows it well." A very convenient abstracted dedication that covers all possible bases, as does "for you, of course" the dedication in Niall Williams' *Only Say the Word.*

Writers need at least one uncritical fan and Bradford F. Swan covered his in his dedication in a book he wrote about Gregory Dexter: "To the memory of my Father because he would have liked Gregory, and to my mother, because every book needs one reader who is going to like it anyhow."

As Bill Clinton's dedication to *My Life* is probably not in the public domain, I'm not going to repeat it verbatim save to say that it covers his mother, his wife, his daughter and his grandfather whom, Clinton intimates "taught me to look up to people others look down on." A fine thing to learn and I must try to restrain any cynical comments on it.

Sometimes the dedications are to people who don't exist such as Aubrey Beardsley's dedication of his manuscript, *Under the Hill* "to the most eminent reverend Prince, Giulo Poldo Pezzoli." This gentleman was a cardinal that Beardsley had invented. I, in my naivety, prefer to think most dedications are to genuine people.

P. G. Wodehouse had considered the matter of dedications rather a lot and announced "I have rather gone off dedications these last forty years or so. To Hell with them about sums up my attitude. Today when I write a book, it's just a book with no trimmings." "I once planned a book," Wodehouse continues, "which was to consist entirely of dedications, but abandoned the idea because I could not think of a dedication for it."

About his dedication in the *Indiscretions of Archie,* Wodehouse wrote to his friend B.W. King-Hall,

My dear Buddy,

We have been friends for eighteen years. A considerable portion of my books were written under your hospitable roof. And yet I have never dedicated one to you. What will the verdict of posterity be on this? The fact is, I have become rather superstitious about dedications. No sooner do you label a book with a legend:

To
My Best Friend X

than X cuts you in Piccadilly, or you bring a lawsuit against him. There is a fatality about it. However I can't imagine anyone quarrelling with you, and I'm getting more attractive all the time, so let's take a chance.

Dedications are not always complimentary. I often dedicate my books to my husband, Elias Wakan, the sculptor, who has been supportive in so many ways that were I to list them, they would read more like an introduction. Once, however, when a show of his sculpture and my book editing coincided, I felt like putting "to Eli, without whom I would have finished this book much faster." Even I could see this was a very mixed compliment and so chose to dedicate it to members of my family (who live thousands of miles away) instead. I noted later a dedication collected by a Bill Morley which included "To Isabel, whose absence ensured the completion of this book," so I didn't feel so guilty after all.

People are not always the focus of a dedication, for example there is the case of Cornell Woolrich who dedicated *The Bride Wore Black* to his typewriter – 'to Remington Portable No. NC 69411 ...' Ah, those Remingtons. And then there is Agatha Christie's dog to whom she dedicated one of her thrillers, "Dear Peter, a dog in a thousand."

The word dedication comes from the Latin *dedicare*, to proclaim, and while they are usually in fairly small print these days, in the case of the muse offering a roof, meals and loving care, many authors should, I feel, perhaps increase the font somewhat in gratitude.

Bill, or more formerly, William F.E. Morley, from whom I quoted above, wrote a great essay on dedications which was, for a while, on the Alcuin Society site, but now seems to have disappeared, as is the way of things on the web. In the essay he lists some dedications from his collection over the years. He divides them into conjugal, clever humility, esoteric, cryptic, patriotic and literary. My favourites among his listing are:

A practical reason for writing – "To my dear sons, Michael and Nicholas, without whose school bills this anthology would not have been made." This was quoted in Dwight Macdonald's anthology, *Parodies*.

The cryptic ones are, however, a bit frustrating "To Katy, who knows why" for example. Then there are the more than self-interested ones such as the dedication in Albert Malvino's book, *Electronic Principles:*

"This book is dedicated to Joanna, my brilliant and beautiful wife without whom I would be nothing. She always comforts and consoles, never complains or interferes, asks nothing, and endures all, and also writes my dedications."

Of course there are always people to take almost any topic to its extreme and so there are trackers of dedications, as Jane Davitt and Tim Morgan did for the more than 100 dedications that Robert Heinlein wrote in his books. Mugglenet, a group of creative young folk, did likewise when they explained all those of J.K. Rowling in her Harry Potter books.

The story of the dedication to Steinbeck's *East of Eden* is particularly fine, as is the dedication itself. Steinbeck's editor for this book was Pascal Covici and, as they say, without the editor, the book would never have got finished. When the 250,000 word manuscript was complete, Steinbeck put it in a mahogany box that he had made and carved and sent it to Covici with the following note on top, which, of course, became the dedication:

> "You came upon me carving some kind of little figure out of wood and you said, "why don't you make something for me?"
> I asked what you wanted and you said, "a box."
> "what for?"
> "to put things in."
> "what things?"
> "whatever you have," you said.
> well, here's your box. Nearly everything I have is in it and it is not full. Pain and excitement are in it, and feeling good or bad and evil thoughts and good thoughts – the pleasure of design and the indescribable joy of creation. And on top of these are all the gratitude and love I have for you and still the box is not full."

A dedication any writer would love to be able to have written.

I dedicated this book to Alice W. Flaherty. I came across her by chance when I was writing the chapter on writer's block. I know little about her, but loved her feisty, cheerful approach to life. She is a neurologist with attitude; just the kind of person brain research needs.

As a post-note, and while it is not a direct dedication within a book, it is still a dedication, the South Burlington Library, Vermont, dedicates a book to each infant of a South Burlington resident. The book is dedicated to the child at birth. The family is notified and the book is placed in the library. What a lovely way to bring a community together around its library. The book could just define the child's life. What book would you have liked to have had donated to your public library at your birth? Mine would have been *Pride and Prejudice,* both of which I am sometimes guilty ... but the romance!

Fan Mail

I write to authors if I like their books. Why not? Writing, as I know only too well, is a solitary job and writers are black holes when it comes to needing reassurance. My letter to the author usually goes something like this:

"Dear Author,

Please forgive me for intruding, but I have just finished your book, ——-, and am overwhelmed with its vision/imagery/language/realism ..."

I then add a few views of my own on the theme of the book and finish with a couple more pats on the back for the author. As a not all together altruistic move, I let them have my website; I'm not sure what they will do with it, or what I want them to do with it ... my fingers just type out www.naomiwakan.com

I usually get a reply by return mail – even from established writers, who have their name above the title on the cover of the book. I get a little shiver of ... I'm not quite sure what, and send some drivel back. At this point the intimate correspondence usually closes because I find it hard to maintain a serious level of praise and concern for very long, for life, and all the activities involved in living (which includes writing fan mail) have always seemed quite ridiculous and inexplicable to me. In one case the author having been over-whelmed by types like me, came up with this message at the bottom of his screen; I nearly missed it:

"To my readers and correspondents: I'm getting swamped with emails again, and it is necessary for me to ask for your cooperation. I will gladly answer urgent, or compelling letters, but please don't overload me with links, clippings, or plain old chitchat. I appreciate your understanding."

Of course the thought that I was neither urgent, nor com-pelling, rather depressed me and so, until I could think of a crucial matter with which to respond, (the author was writing about the end of the world as we know it, when our oil supply runs out) I decide to let sleeping dogs lie.

Still I didn't regret writing. Carolyn See in her fine book *Making a Literary Life: Advice for Writers and Other Dreamers*, tells how she never wrote to E.M. Forster about how A *Room with a View* and *The Longest Journey* changed her life. There is a wonderful passage where she tells of these regrets:

"There had been months, even years, when I could have written him a note to say thank you. Thank you for reminding me I'm not totally alone on this earth; thank you for teaching me about morality and passion in a way I can respect: thanks for teaching me that profound looks better against a background of violets that 'spot the grass with azure foam.'"

Now you don't want to have those kind of regrets, do you? When you love the words you're reading, tell the writer.

Yes, as a writer I too get fan mail; among the recent letters received – one from India and two from the northern UK, and an indignant one from Vancouver asking me how I could justify charging Cdn $50 for a 2-1/2 hour writing workshop. I actually replied in detail to this one and by the time I had added up all the things needed in the preparation, booking and getting participants for a workshop, the money had dwindled to $2 an hour. I felt better. I don't know what my indignant correspondent felt, because I never heard from her again.

Fans often slip the odd poem in for critiquing and I slip back a reference to my editing fees without commenting on their enclosed verse in the style of Robbie Burns, haiku of strictly five, seven, five syllables (Ugh!), poems about doggie/pussy-cat/horse, etc. I guess that does seem a bit ungenerous when I read of fan letters that result in a contract because the author has recommended the fan's work to his agent.

There is a wonderful story of a young boy who wrote a fan letter to a baseball player. Fifteen years later he got a reply. The baseball player had put a couple of hundred fan mail letters in a box when he moved house. The box went into the garage, and we all know what that means. When his wife indicated it was time to clear the garage out, the baseball player discovered the box and, now retired, had lots of time to write replies including the one to the 10 year old boy, who was now a man. The story is very touching and you can read it completely by searching out *The Autograph Man* by Bryan Curtis.

People don't just write fan mail to the living. I'm sure Elvis and even Rudolph Valentino still get letters. Fictional people have their share too, as letters pour in to Baker Street for Sherlock Holmes and to television stations for various characters (rather than the actors playing them).

As I mentioned the sort of fan letter I write, I began to wonder whether there is a standard form with recommendations to be adhered to. I can only suggest you never use an author's first name when addressing them. Unless you know them personally, I think that maybe stepping in a little closer than most writers would appreciate. I would make my praise real and specific. Writers like to know what works and what doesn't for their readers. My husband, when he writes to authors, tends to point out typographical errors in their work, which he has already marked in pencil. He can probably get away with this because his letters are so 'real,' but I wouldn't recommend wasting time doing what the publisher must have already had done, ready for the next print run.

If you just praise the author, all they can do is say "Thank you." If you want to continue a correspondence, it is good to find mutual ground, maybe even outside the topics that the author's book covers. Why should the writer reply to you if you haven't raised a question they are interested in, or referred them to a book, or website, that might be useful? The writer will reply, if they are polite, but will only continue the letter exchange if it's in their interest. If you keep them on a pedestal, you will never get a letter from a human being. More probably it will be from their staff, or a willingly-recruited mother, and, once more, it will be a formal "Thank you."

As a young housewife, I spent my reading hours on psychology books and, because of an interest in the mind, on telepathy. At that time, a certain Professor Lethbridge was writing on the subject, and I sent him a fan letter. I must have introduced topics of mutual interest, because our correspondence continued for some years. I read all his books and offered suggestions that must have been supportive. Unfortunately no letters remain from this correspondence because I am not a hoarder. Still, looking back, I can see how a fan can become a friend by not idolizing, but by offering support and help. My correspondent was Thomas Charles Lethbridge, Director of Excavations for the Cambridge

Antiquarian Society and for the University Museum of Archaeology and Ethnology. I only knew him as someone who was interested in dream telepathy, as I was, and who could make statements such as, "The brain is a method for censoring sensation," which I found very exciting at the time.

Oddly enough authors seem to find their 'hate' fan mail much better written than their 'love' fan mail. I suppose the fact that love softens everything into a generalized slush, whereas hate focuses energy into a piercing laser, could explain this, or is this only my fanciful interpretation?

Of course, if you are a writer, you will know that fan mail cannot possibly represent a picture of your total readership for only people who seriously love your work or seriously hate your work will bother to write. I like to imagine that the bulk of my readership lies somewhere in between liking it enough to buy it, and, if they hate it, not enough to bother telling me so.

By the way, it is good manners to send author's fan mail via their agent, or publisher, rather than directly to them, (unless, of course, you know them personally), otherwise it might be considered a literary form of stalking. But, as I mentioned, lonely authors (and film stars come to that) often have an email address on their website inviting contact. The reply may, however, be a little indirect, as in the case of Patti Smith who tells that her mother answers all her fan mail!

Sometimes I write lengthy letters and never receive answers, not knowing, indeed whether they have ever been received. I usually keep copies of all such correspondence, as, being rather practical, I may be able to incorporate them into a piece later on, and so the writing time would not have been a complete waste. I once wrote a wonderful letter to John Le Carré telling him how I read all his spy stories in the process of making a rather flamboyant quilt, and how the greyness of the fog-filled cities of Smiley's people contrasted with the reds and oranges of my crazy quilt. He never replied and so I used the piece in an essay on how to write about arts and crafts.

Some celebrities just have no way of being contacted and make it clear. The Rolling Stones web site says "no, we do not forward fan mail, or answer fan mail to the Rolling Stones. The Stones have no email address, or otherwise, for receiving fan mail." I am an unfocused person, by nature, but when I make up my mind to thank someone, I do it, whether they want to receive my thanks, or not. Recently I read an uproariously funny piece called *Jane Eyre runs for President* by a Mr. Sean Carman. His site showed no way of contacting him and, although I knew that by day he was a lawyer, I felt going via the office would be tricky. You can never tell with lawyers. I did, however, find another site for whom he occasionally wrote and so addressed my copious praise to him via that site. I have no idea whether it will ever be forwarded to him. That was not the point in this instance. I just needed to thank the universe for making me laugh out loud on a trying morning.

In my letter to Mr. Carman I invited him to sail up to visit us (don't all lawyers have yachts?) and indicated which marina he should anchor at. Who knows, lawyers have to rest sometime and perhaps he, in particular, would like to rest with us on Gabriola. Of course, his humour may not run off the page into the person, but that's a risk I'm willing to take.

I love the blog of a new writer, Hilary Moon Murphy, who says, "I am up to twelve pieces of fan mail now. I'm not tired of it yet. If you like my stuff, let me know. I do respond to all my fan mail and I'd love to hear from you." When her books start to pile up and the fan mail starts to get unreasonably large, she may not feel quite the same. However, it is lovely to enjoy the beginning process with her.

Blogs, of course, generate their own fan mail. In fact I would think that the web has multiplied the sending of fan mail by the million. In my researching for this chapter, I accidentally dropped into hundreds of blogs and chat rooms where compliments (and heavy derogatory comments in language I was unable to recognize) were flying around.

Some writers, while welcoming fan mail, specify what they do not want to receive. This includes jokes, viruses, petitions, lewd inquiries, or lewd mail of any sort. Other 'do-nots' include, do not ask the author to meet you, call you, comment on your manuscript, or marry you. Authors do not have time for such activities and anyway may not be looking for a bride or groom at this moment.

A little prepared filtering can go a long way. I would add that I also don't want to receive enquiries from my fans as to how they can get their work published, or whether they can come and stay for an unspecified length of time. I'm happy to have them drop by casually for tea, although since I live at the extreme end of an island two ferry rides away from Vancouver, I'm not quite sure how that casualness could possibly happen.

Epilogue

A Voice for the Ages

People use the phrase 'it's not writing for the ages,' very much as they use the phrase 'it's not rocket science.' They mean in both cases, that a thing is not hard to do, nor hard to understand. However, although writing for the ages does demand writing with clarity, simplicity and integrity, I think it is not beyond the average writer. Richard Feynman, I believe, once said that you should be able to express a thing you know in one paragraph, and that, perhaps, is what I mean – not necessarily brevity, although many wise one-line sayings have survived the years, but clear, concise writing. Of course, Feynman expressed his profound ideas all in one simple diagram, but then that was Feynman.

'Writing with your own voice' is another intimidating phrase, which it shouldn't be. Writing with one's own voice is a necessary element of writing for the ages, and is something most writers achieve, sooner or later. It is not so much 'finding' your voice, for you never lost it, it is more like retrieving it from the layers of rubble, concepts, rules, and inhibitions under which it has been hidden.

Retrieving one's voice is an inner process; a process of trying, and a process of discarding … discarding until a perfect match between the inner and the outer is obtained such that what you want to say in your head matches what is said on the page. Of course that perfect match is rarely achieved, but when the blend is almost seamless, the voice rings through true, as the writer's outer trappings have dropped away leaving their essence to shine.

A writer's voice is hard to define. Perhaps it is better defined by what it's not; it's not style, nor wit, nor perfect grammar, nor wisdom. Perhaps integrity defines it best; the integrity of someone no longer playing games, no longer having to cover-up, no longer parrying and sparring with life, someone coming straight through.

Writers worry a lot about losing their voice. They read previous things they have written in wonder, and ponder whether they will ever be able to write that way again. Even experienced writers also have such moments of concern.

For a writer not trying to write for the ages, it is still important to use your true writing voice, for it sets your readers at ease. Because there is no posturing when you write this way, they are able to read you directly, as through a glass lightly. However there are times when you are writing that your mind wanders off, when you stop paying attention to your own words spilling on to the screen, when you have lost the rhythm of what you are writing. It is then you know, for sure, that the reader will also stop paying attention, and that somehow you have lost your voice and drifted away from yourself.

What things stifle a writer's voice? Writing for the market can mute the voice, for with success comes the desire to repeat success, and then watch how quickly integrity morphs into formula and a fresh voice vanishes. How to keep the hubris that often comes with fame, or even with the publication of one slender book, from smothering your voice is an ever present problem.

The way I look at it is that you have something you need to tell and someone to whom you need to tell it. The need is urgent, so urgent that you have no time to make it palatable, pleasurable to a certain group of people, or marketable – you just have time to get it out. It's as simple (and as difficult) as that. If you wish to maintain your voice, my advice is to get out of the way and let the writing proceed; the writing that is meant for the reader only. That does not mean that you somehow float off and let the writing write itself, as I described above, for that can become mindless writing. What I aim for is for the writing to write itself whilst I, somehow, stay beside it, alert and focused, and a clear channel. If I get distracted by writing to please my writing group, my publisher, or my critics, the channel will somehow block, my voice muddy, and what comes out may be somebody's stuff, but it won't be mine.

Having a voice doesn't mean that all your writing has to come out in a particular style. If it does, it might mean that you have typecast your writing, rather like an actor gets typecast. The danger there is that you might become a parody of yourself. Your writing voice should be as familiar to you as any part of your body, and while it is the one you use for writing, you can choose to use it speedily, or slowly, with bravura or with contemplation just as you can use your speaking voice to exhort, to protest, to calm or to love.

Writers are often warned about being influenced by too much praise when they have just discovered their own voice and it is still a little wobbly:

"If people praise you, you are not walking your own path."
– David Mitchell

This doesn't mean, of course, that if you are being true to your own voice, you can't receive praise. You certainly can. The danger is that the praise will become so loud that your own voice may wander slightly off course. It would not be the first time this has happened in the history of writing.

Too much praise is not the only thing that can corrupt. Grading and ranking has somewhat the same effect. How can one grade writing?

Danger!

When I hear of a contest,
a competition, prizes –
first, second, third
and honourable mention,
particularly when I hear
"honourable mention,"
I close all notebooks
scattered around the house
and shut my pens and pencils
away fast in a tight box.
I resist submitting
a life-threatening poem,
lest the thought
of first, second, third
and honourable mention
divide me from myself ...
a substance hardly won.

Voice has lots to do with communicating beyond concepts, beyond barriers. It is also about reaching across cultures and between generations. It is an element, as I said above, in writing for the ages.

You can write for your family, your friends, your social milieu, the readers of the 21st century, the baby-boomers etc., but if you want to write for the ages, you'll have to dig a little deeper. Not more sophisticated – that will only trap you in intellectual concepts – but simpler. Start by trying to find the small voice of yourself at say, age eight, the tiny voice that could only state what it saw. That will bring you closer to writing words that will survive.

A poet who describes a poet's moment and does not draw the reader in deeper to make it a universal moment, is not writing for the ages. When I give workshops about writing haiku, I often ask my students to write a paragraph, then precis it to three lines describing what subject they are talking about, where it is happening and when. When they have cut things down to three sentences, I ask them to cut out all unnecessary words, personal references and cultural terms that are local and not shared by other cultures. What is left is a very intense image that in its great simplicity touches deep inside and opens one to the ends of the universe. That is writing for the ages.

Oh dear! Why am I telling you all this, and offering all these enigmatic definitions, and making all these impossible demands, when all you really want to do is tell me how the plum tree looks, when the shadows lengthen and the blossoms stand out stark? Well yes, then we are agreed. If you tell me *exactly* that, in exactly the words you want to use to convey it, then that is exactly what I want to hear and what I mean by all the above nonsense.

Opinions seem to differ widely on which books have been written that will survive the passage of time. These books have nothing to do with sales figures, although the Christian Bible, being the number one bestseller of all times, is also listed in some people's most important books of all times. *Don Quixote* ranks on most lists, as does *The Pilgrim's Progress* and *Gulliver's Travels*. Closer to our times, *Wuthering Heights*, *Jane Eyre* and *Vanity Fair* appear frequently, and into the 20th century *Ulysses* by James Joyce is listed, but how many people have actually read it? The same goes for Proust's *In Search of Lost Time*. Few would exclude Tolstoy's *War and Peace* and *The Brothers Karamazov* (Dostoevsky), but when we come to books written within the last fifty years, the lists fall apart and there seems to be far less agreement.

My projected list of books that have been written in the last fifty years that will last at least another fifty, include *A Fine Balance* by Rohinton Mistry and *To Kill a Mockingbird* by Harper Lee. As I read far more non-fiction than fiction I would add *The Lives of a Cell* by Lewis Thomas, *Six Easy Pieces* by Richard Feynman, *Pilgrim at Tinker Creek* by Anne Dillard, *Silent Spring* by Rachel Carson, and, perhaps *Longitude* by Dava Sobel. I suppose I could easily add another twenty. The factors these books all have in common are decency, honesty (as far as the facts could be ascertained), vision, integrity and the earnestness to say what needed to be said at the time the book was written.

I should also add, what, for me, in my poet's robe, is a very important piece of writing that has been reproduced many, many times. It is e e cummings reply to a high school editor and was first published in the Ottawa Hills (Grand Rapids, Michigan) High School *Spectator* October 26th, 1955. Yes, I have squeezed it in under the fifty year limit because it is the best advice any budding poet could wish for. It can be read in *Cummings: A Miscellany* and will still be being read 100 years from now, if humans, and poets, are still around at that time.

And while we're talking about writing that lasts down the ages, and I still have in mind my workshop exercise, I vaguely recall a story, (I think it might be by Borges, but haven't managed to track it down) that empowers one word as much as a word can be empowered. That word is becoming central to my philosophy, as it is to others, so never mind writing that will still have impact 100 years from now, here's the tale of a single word that I hope will still be around then.

"A king once had a whim, as kings do, and asked his wise men to gather all the books of the kingdom, which contained all the wisdom of the kingdom, in one place in the palace. This they were able to do. The king then asked them to precis each book down to one chapter. The wise men protested, but as the alternative was to lose their heads (literally), they had little option. Within some days it was done. The king then asked the wise men to put the precis chapters together and then precis the precis down to one paragraph. Again there were protests from the wise men, but, considering the alternative, they eventually produced one paragraph. The king smiled a little and then asked for the paragraph to be defined by one sentence. The wise men had pretty well given up by then and quickly produced a sentence. The king at last expressed a little approval and said "Fine! Now give to me all the wisdom of the kingdom in one word!"

What was the word? My students, on hearing the tale, have suggested it was 'love,' 'intelligence,' 'nonsense,' 'light,' etc., but actually the word was 'maybe.'

Unfortunately writing for the ages is not something that can be taught, but I don't want to leave you with the feeling that it is an impossible goal towards which you should struggle all your writing life. In the final piece in the book, "A Plea for Kindness," you'll be glad to hear that I moderate my demands somewhat. I still ask for integrity in the books which I read, for generosity, for tolerance, but I also ask for that badly needed, and hard to define quality, kindness. Is that too much to ask?

A Plea for Kindness

It may seem strange to write about kindness when one is considering the writing process and the publishing world. Writing is a demanding, lonely process, in which the words only occasionally flow smoothly and are much more likely to have to be torn from the soul. No kindness in the process at all. More like a story of the life of a stoical hermit locked in his cell, or that of the brutality of a bar-jumping lush who has to get sozzled before he or she can utter a word of truth.

As to publishers they may not intend to be cruel, but the need to select a few titles from so many submissions demands efficiency and perhaps curtness towards the author. As to the critics they depend for an income on trashing a book in the wittiest way they can. Even moderate critics have to catch the public interest if their copy is not to cause a drooping of the eyelids.

Now how to introduce kindness into this milieu, for kindness is what is demanded in a world that often seems full of irritation, friction and despair.

Writers, please have the kindness to at least pay attention to the publisher's guidelines. They don't establish them for nothing. It is the preferred way they like to receive submissions and the way it makes their work easier. Making their work easier is surely what you want to do as a writer, that is, if you want to get a contract. An attractive, and obedient submission, will not receive an out-of-hand rejection without even a glance, I can almost assure you. Clean pages, paginated, with requested line space and your name and that of the manuscript in the top right-hand corner are a small price to pay to get past immediately being thrown on the reject pile. However good your work (in your estimation) you will still have to fit in with the publisher's practice when the contract is received and editing commences ... might as well start being pleasant at the time you send in your submission.

To you publishers, writing a book, however gauche, or gross, it may be, still requires enormous output of effort and much soul-searching. While you may not require the soul to be searched quite that much, the effort put out by the author deserves recognition. Printed rejection letters are so cold; why not at least have a name attached so that one can tell that a robot hasn't been employed. The few words, "try us again" if you see promise, or "good luck" can turn a writer's cloudy day into one with a pale ray of future hope. You, of course, are not legally responsible for the author's reaction to your rejection, but a little kindness could produce, at long odds, a Dostoevsky.

Critics, be clever without intellectual pretences, and witty without using the author as a sitting duck for your brilliance. If you are free-lancing you could choose books that resonate with you and therefore can be kind because you are full of admiration. If you are handed a manuscript in your line of work with no way of slipping it onto someone else's desk, remember that any book is a human being's energy. It may be wasted in your opinion, but it is still energy ... a reaching out, a need to communicate. The reaching may not be appealing and the communication better repressed, but some acknowledgement of those days at the writing desk should still be recognized with, perhaps, an odd kind word without it destroying your integrity, fame or income.

Darwinian rivalries, jockeying for power and fame happen in all spheres of life. Being in the book world myself I have to let out at least a tiny plea for a little more civility, a little more courtesy. A little more kindness.

Naomi Beth Wakan has written over thirty books including *Images of Japan, Segues* and *Late Bloomer: On Writing Later in Life.* Her title, *Haiku – one breath poetry* was an American Library Association selection. She is a member of The League of Canadian Poets, Haiku Canada and Tanka Canada. Her essays, haiku and tanka have appeared in many magazines and anthologies and she is included in *The Canadian Haiku Anthology,* Spring 2008. Naomi lives on Gabriola Island with her husband, the sculptor, Elias Wakan.